The JEWISH ATHLETES HALL OF FAME

by

Buddy Robert S. Silverman, Ph.D

Shapolsky Publishers, Inc.
New York, N.Y.

For additional information, contact:
Shapolsky Publishers, Inc.
136 West 22nd Street
New York, NY 10011
212/633-2022   FAX 212/633-2123

First Edition 1989

10 9 8 7 6 5 4 3 2 1

Library of Congress Cataloging-in-Publication

Silverman, Buddy Robert S.
    The jewish athletes hall of fame / Buddy Robert S. Silverman.
    p. cm.
Summary: Surveys the accomplishments and struggles of outstanding Jewish
    American athletes and sports team owners, managers, and coaches.
1. Jewish athletes-United States-Biography-Juvenile literature. [1. Athletes.
2. Jews-United States-Biography.]
 I. Title

GV697.A1S52 1989   796.089'924'073-dc20   89-32618

ISBN 0-944007-04-x

Manufactured in the United States of America

ACKNOWLEDGMENTS

Inspiration to complete The Jewish Athletes Hall of Fame came out of my perception of dwindling interest among Jewish people with supporting Zionism or perpetuating their legacy; and the will of one person to do something about it with his life's work in the most magnified way possible, through the written word. That person is Ian Shapolsky, publisher of Shapolsky Books--books that collectively serve as an everlasting inspiration to support Zionism and perpetuate the Jewish legacy.

During the course of writing this book, I suffered the ultimate loss--that of my father, who was also my best friend. Although my goal of naming a son Abraham (Al) George Silverman II after him may be overtaken by a biological clock, the fact that my Jewish Athletes Hall of Fame has finally come to fruition is something that I know he would have liked. This book is dedicated to Colonel Abraham George Silverman, J.D. -- an honorary member of The Jewish Athletes Hall of Fame. Because he elected to attend Massachusetts Institute of Technology and then Brooklyn Law School, no one will ever know how great a second baseman he might have been.

Earlier in the course of writing this book, I suffered the losses of Bogie, a pedigreed miniature black-haired poodle; Pompo, a pedigreed miniature black-haired poodle; and Buddy, a pedigreed collie for whom I am now named. I have also recognized the losses of Stroupie, a pedigreed spitz; Honey, a pedigreed cocker spaniel; and Blackie, a short-haired dog of mixed stock. To them and to all homeless dogs subjected to slaughter and experimentation, I also dedicate this book.

Finally, the credit for motivating me to complete this work belongs to my family--Clara L. Silverman, my mother, who is still an ardent golfer; my partner, Lady Pompie, a pedigreed collie who is Buddy's grandniece and Pompo's namesake; and Cappuccino, a toy white-haired poodle who keeps the memory of my father's gentleness toward him alive.

Buddy Robert S. Silverman, Ph.D
1989

COLONEL ABRAHAM (AL) GEORGE SILVERMAN, J.D.

PREFACE

To the Jewish people who were tortured to death at Auschwitz, at Buchenwald, at Dachau, at Mauthausen, at Sachsenhausen, and at Treblinka—all six million of them—this book is dedicated.

This book is also dedicated to the elite of Israel's athletic team who died a violent death during the 1972 Olympics in the country responsible for those six million deaths, but this time at the hands of Arab terrorists—terrorists who would be released by Germany, in a bitter twist of nostalgia, back to their homeland. Three decades had passed since Germany had completed its Final Solution of the Jewish Problem, but in 1972 the results were the same: Mark Slavin, 18, a wrestler, dead; Elizer Halfin, 24, a wrestler, dead; Andre Spitzer, 27, a fencing coach, dead; David Berger, 28, a weight lifter, dead; Ze'ev Friedman, 32, a weight lifter, dead; Joseph Romano, 32, a weight lifter, dead; Moshe Weinberg, 32, a wrestling coach, dead; Amitzur Shapira, 40, a track and field coach, dead; Yosef Gottfreund, 40, a wrestling referee, dead; Ya'acov Springer, 52, a weight lifting referee, dead; and Kehat Shorr, 53, a shooting coach, dead. Adding insult to injury, then International Olympic Committee President Avery Brundage denied Israel's request to stop the olympiad at that point in honor of the dead. To these victims of terrorism and to the thousands of other Jewish victims of terrorism, this book is also dedicated.

Also, this book is dedicated to Nazi hunter Simon Wiesenthal, who directed the 1960 capture and subsequent execution in Israel of Adolf Eichmann; and to attorney Louis Marshall, who brought Henry Ford, America's number-one automobile tycoon and anti-Semite, to his knees during the twenties by leading an unprecedented boycott of his automobiles by individual Jews, Jewish firms, and gentile firms dependent upon Jewish trade. Their willingness to assume the role of defenders of Jewish rights and their success in attracting the necessary support of Jewish people has made them role models for all famous Jewish people with a desire to use their prominence in protecting Jewish interests.

After the Munich murders, I set out to establish this Jewish Athletes Hall of Fame as a memorial to the slain Israeli Olympic Team members. Over the next two years, I had been in personal contact with nearly all of the major Jewish sports figures to draw out their thoughts on substantive issues affecting Jews in sports. But, in a letter to me dated September 9, 1974, I was requested by a prominent Jewish athlete not to include him in my Jewish Sports Hall of Fame out of reasons connected with his personal security and the potential threat of terrorism. Out of concern over the possibility that my work might indeed make any of the athletes a target, I made the announcement that I was suspending my efforts to start a Jewish Sports Hall of Fame. Five years later, a totally unrelated Jewish Sports Hall of Fame was established in Israel; and four years after that, another publisher released a compendium of biographies on Jewish athletes. In both cases, that particular Jewish athlete attracted substantial coverage without offering any apparent opposition or suffering any adverse consequences. It was only then that I resumed my work. Because much of my previously unpublished exclusive correspondence is dated almost 15 years ago, some of the Jewish sports figures who wrote me have since passed away. This book is dedicated to them as well.

I have devoted my life not only to remembrance of Jewish martyrs, but also to animal rights—upon whom daily slaughter, vivisection, and other experimentation are a tragic revisitation of the Holocaust. To all of the helpless animals subjected to slaughter or experimentation, I also dedicate this book.

During the course of writing this book, I suffered the ultimate loss—that of my father, who was also my best friend. Although my goal of naming a son Abraham (Al) George Silverman II after him may eventually be overtaken by a biological clock, the fact that my Jewish Sports Hall of Fame has finally come to fruition is something that I know he would have liked. This book is especially dedicated to Col. Abraham (Al) George Silverman, J.D.—an honorary member of the Jewish Sports Hall of Fame.

To the hundreds of famous and supportive individuals who contributed their time, thoughts, or valuable photographs to this effort, my indebtedness can never be fully repaid. Thank you very much.

Finally, the credit for inspiring me to complete this work belongs to my mother, Clara L. Silverman, who is still an ardent golfer.

Buddy Robert S. Silverman, Ph.D.
1989

CONTENTS

The Jewish-American
All-Time Sports Executive Rankings

The
JEWISH
ATHLETES
HALL OF FAME

INTRODUCTION

The date was March 11, 1988. The medium was network television. Suddenly, two faces emerged on the television screen positioned strategically opposite from a third face to denote an obvious conflict of opinion. Aligned together were a recognizable Jewish movie actor and the literary editor of a politically oriented magazine. Placed alone was the Israeli Ambassador to the United Nations. At issue was Israel's forcefully resilient stand against violent Palestinians protesting Zionism. The famous movie actor and literary editor had gained attention by taking a virtually unprecedented stand as American Jews against policies of the State of Israel. The moderator raised questions regarding whether their sentiment reflected a lessened support of Israel by the collective body of American Jews. The Israeli Ambassador seemed alone in his expressed views justifying the defensive measures employed by the Jewish State and its reluctance to relinquish land or negotiate with terrorists.

Suddenly, a fourth face appeared beside that of the Israeli Ambassador. It was a famous Jewish athlete proclaiming support of Israel and approval of her policies. The message conveyed to the American public by the actor and editor no longer appeared to necessarily represent a broad consensus.

Unfortunately that was not the way it happened. No fourth person ever appeared on the television screen. No famous Jewish athlete came forward. Not that time. But, the potential for this to happen is ever present; because the number of former and existing Jewish athletes prominent enough to demand that type of exposure and generate that type of impact is staggering.

The Jewish superstar exerts an irresistible attraction for the American Jew by symbolizing ethnic heroes responsible for Israel's unremitting and successful physical battle for survival. Prominence of Jewish individuals in the arts and sciences had created a weakling Jewish stereotype resistant even to the triumphs of indestructible Israel. Now entrenched in the public eye as representative of a competitive people, the Jew in American sports effectively divorces American Jewry from the debilitated image as "Momma's boys" and weaklings. With last names often serving as reminders of their ethnic origin and an enlightened media recognizing their numbers, Jewish athletes transfer their acclaim to American Jewry because of the public's tendency to judge a whole people's caliber on the physical prowess of some of their most gifted individuals.

In each prominent Jewish athlete, American Jewry has a potentially visible spokesperson capable of influencing a sports-dominated society about critical Jewish issues. Regardless of the individual's decision concerning whether to lend his or her name in other than a sports arena, that athlete's professional acclaim can inexplicably be inferred as political approval by the public of positions supporting Jewish interests. Because of this the Jewish athlete faces a threat of terrorism nonexistent to other athletes.

Fighting under the name Benny Leonard, Benjamin Leiner molded the boxing style made famous by Cassius Clay. Leonard lent his name freely for Jewish causes the way Clay would as Muhammad Ali fifty years later for his fellow blacks. Benny Leonard held the World Lightweight Boxing Championship for almost a decade in the teens and twenties. He died without knowing his legendary career would some day help shatter the stereotype embarrassing American Jewry.

Although considered in the teens as the greatest guard in professional basketball history, Nat Holman saved his most important contribution toward collective Jewish dignity until some fifty years later. As president of the United States Committee on Sports for Israel, he sponsored what would become permanent, comprehensive, physical education and fitness programs for all Israeli youth. Holman emphasized that the outstanding performance of Jewish athletes has a profound effect on Jewish youth and adults as well as on non-Jews. "Excellence in sports helps Jews to be even prouder of their great heritage so that they can keep their heads high without feeling inferior to any other group. It is a major responsibility of all prominent Jewish athletes to dedicate themselves to partnership with the best interests and highest ideals of Jewish life," Holman maintained.

Benny Friedman introduced the passing game to college football in the twenties. It earned him an early spot in the College Football Hall of Fame. "Jews naturally look to those who are outstanding in a sport and identify with them. But, in athletics there is a common denominator of dedication to a team that transcends all else. One gives and takes and performs and is recognized by his performance, not by any outside circumstances," Friedman said.

In less than three years, Andy Cohen's brilliant baseball career came to an abrupt end. New York needed a Jewish athlete to attract its Jewish constituents and the New York Giants baseball team needed a second baseman to replace traded Hall-of-Famer Rogers Hornsby. The pressure proved too great. "The label 'Great Jewish Hope' did inflict pressure. There were times I tried too hard. I considered myself a representative of Jewish fans. The tremendous publicity and the fact I played so well in my first game helped cause prejudice from players as well as fans," Cohen said. Andy's brother Syd pitched briefly in the twenties, during the time Andy drew banner newspaper headlines by his mere presence. "Neither Andy nor I ever played ball on either Rosh Hashanah or Yom Kippur. Our wonderful mother told us people would have more respect for Jews by our not working on these special days," Syd Cohen said.

Lou Gordon emerged as a consensus All-America tackle at the University of Illinois. "I was not necessarily aware of any special following from Jewish fans. I considered myself an individual player and felt no obligation to stand up and act as a representative for the fans in matters of social interest," Gordon said.

Five prime years away from baseball in heavy combat during the second World War did little to diminish what still amounted to one of the most spectacular of all sports careers. Hank Greenberg earned distinction as a slugger in the class of Babe Ruth. He surfaced again in his sixties as perennial champion of the annual Dewar's Sports Celebrity Tennis Tournament. "Like all civilized people, I was shocked by the tragedy at Munich. In this current world atmosphere—where tragic events take place daily—one must continue to live as though these happenings do not take place," Greenberg said.

Sid Luckman introduced the T formation into professional football and dominated the sport during the darkest hours in Jewish history. "My talents were strictly athletic and whenever called upon to speak publicly, it was always in relation to my sport and the people connected with it. As athletes, I don't think we are qualified or well enough informed to voice opinion on grave issues," Luckman said.

Unlike Sid Luckman, Marshall Goldberg never lived up to the promise of his college days in professional football. But, the running turned defensive back played on a championship team at the twilight of his career. "I am too engrossed in my present activities to think about history. My place in American sports was created many years ago and the final chapter was written in 1948," Marshall Goldberg said.

Dolph Schayes took the name Adolph out of the gutter and made it an adjective for precision in basketball during the fifties. The ambidextrous forward established himself as the most explosive threat in professional basketball until the days of seven-foot centers in the next decade. "Obviously, American Jews take pride in accomplishments of successful Jewish athletes, not only on a national level but down the line in high school. Public opinion is influenced by attention getters—whether they be athletes, clergymen, or politicians—speaking intelligently on any issue," Schayes said.

In the fifties, Major League Baseball—for the second time—reached a unanimous selection of Most Valuable Player: Al Rosen. Hank Greenberg had been the first Jewish player to earn that distinction. When the slugging third baseman retired, he appeared an obvious candidate for baseball's Hall of Fame. He will now have to wait years for an old-timers committee to consider his rejected record. "It is incumbent upon Jews everywhere to become well-known spokesmen for the Jewish religion. I feel that Jewish athletes, particularly because of the publicity given to their acts, should always be aware of their heritage and act accordingly," Rosen said.

An arthritic elbow forced an early end to one of the most spectacular pitching careers in baseball history. Sandy Koufax stunned the people of America in 1965. He sat out the first game of the World Series in observance of the Jewish Day of Atonement, Yom Kippur. Eight years later, public recognition of Yom Kippur's sanctity surfaced in horror at the now famous assault on Israel that day. Two years later, a Maryland high school coach received highly publicized discipline for holding football practice on Yom Kippur for his football team—a team without any Jewish players. "My personal feelings have always remained private and I would prefer to keep it that way," Koufax said.

As Sandy Koufax compiled a record book of strikeout and no-hit precedents, The Intellectual Assassin—also known as Ron Mix—earned recognition as one of the greatest offensive linemen in professional football history. "The general feeling is that physical prowess and intellectual accomplishment are mutually exclusive. It has been part of the Jewish stereotype to equate Jews with intellectuals, not with physical prowess," Mix said. "Well," he added, "Jews take the same pride in physical accomplishment as others and thus have been undoubtedly troubled by this phase of their stereotype—just as they have been troubled by other phases. So, the Jew is likely to have a racial pride in the accomplishments of a Jewish athlete. I witnessed this during my career. Witness the great pride world Jewry takes in accomplishments of Israel and in the collective Israeli reputation for hard work, fighting, courage, and daring. The emergence of Israel has completely changed the stereotype of the Jew and allowed him to function comfortably in American society."

As an unheralded Maccabiah (Israel's Jewish Olympics) veteran in 1964, Marilyn Ramenofsky emerged as the top ranking 400-meter women's freestyle swimmer in the world. She broke world records three times, capturing an Olympic silver medal along the way. "Stricter security measures could have been taken for the Israeli athletes and coaches in light of incidents prior to the tragedy. I feel greatly embittered. But, the true crisis of the Munich Olympics is its evolution away from the original intent of athletic competition," Ramenofsky said. She explained that the Olympics historically displaced political hostilities in favor of pure competition, but not now. "The modern Games breed extreme nationalism, which results in the epitome of violent extremism. There were intermediate steps that set the stage. I witnessed these intermediate steps. In the 1964 Olympic village at Tokyo, the U.S. officials and coaches were extremely cognizant of winning gold medals and freely imparted their values to their athletes. I felt that the personality of American youth was not being clearly represented by these American officials, who were caught up in the political importance of the Olympics and not particularly interested in international communication. There are many more medals given in swimming than in gymnastics. So, how can medal accumulation in a particular sport indicate national strength?" she said.

Leg injuries constraining his speed and accuracy around the goal prevented former Israeli Olympic soccer team captain Roby Young from achieving his promise for the American New York Cosmos team. "I think Jewish athletes should use their prominence to exert influence on public opinion and to change any image of an unathletic Jew. Whether to play in Germany or not is a long-term argument in Israel. My feelings are that we should play there in order to prove that the nation of Israel is alive. Yet, we should never forget what their parents have done to our nation and to the world. I would play there and try to play my best ever. I never had a chance to play in Russia; Israel played Russia in 1956 at Moscow. I would play there for one reason: to lift the morale of the Jews of Russia. The Israeli flag and the national anthem in the stadium would do it," Young said.

As a rookie, Kenny Holtzman handed Sandy Koufax his last regular season pitching defeat. Herman Franks, former Giant manager managed against both Koufax and Holtzman many times. "Holtzman should follow Koufax into the Hall of Fame," Franks said. Although not as spectacular as Koufax on the mound, Holtzman contributed as much toward world Jewry as any athlete before him. "The night I learned about Munich was the night before I was to pitch in Chicago. I was with Mike Epstein and—needless to say—we were shocked. I think we felt angry at first and then grief. We knew some crackpot could be after one of us," Holtzman said. "We decided to wear black armbands the next day at the game, although neither of us felt like playing. We wore the bands for about a week," he added, "realizing this could mark us. But, it didn't matter. Nobody feels the sting of prejudice like some professional athletes. One day—when I'm out of the game—I'll tell it like it was."

Swimmer Mark Spitz escaped Arab terrorists who killed 11 members of the Israeli Olympic team at the 1972 Munich Olympiad after winning seven gold medals. Edward Rosenblum also witnessed the tragedy. The Munich Games marked the sixth olympiad Rosenbloom had attended as a representative of the United States. In 1958, Edward Rosenblum organized the first visit by a United States track and field team to Russia. "The Jewish-American athlete in association and competition with his non-Jewish athlete was the formation and monumental beginning to better understanding and a more harmonious relation between the two groups. A Jewish-American athlete (Spitz) was heralded as the greatest athlete in Munich for his performance as a swimmer. We all felt the Munich Games would be the best ever held," Rosenblum said.

Soon after the Munich murders, Israel continued sending teams abroad. The Israel National Basketball team competed in the World Student Games in Moscow and mobs physically attacked the Russian Jewish supporters. Coach Avraham Hemmo recalled how Kenny Holtzman, in particular, and other Jewish athletes publicly protested the Munich murders. "We were aware Holtzman and the others felt for their brothers who died in Munich. We go anywhere in the world to play. We prove we're not afraid. We want to live like anyone has a right to live. We won't stay home afraid. All of us are fighters from the front," Hemmo said.

Counterpunching Harold Solomon relied on pinpoint control to emerge among the top 10 ranked tennis players in the world. "I was appalled at what took place in Munich; and there can never be any justification for actions that took place in Germany before that," Solomon said. He recalled the severe security precautions forced upon Jewish athletes during the Davis Cup match in Romania after the summer of 1972. "The entire airfield was surrounded by soldiers with machine guns. The secret service came up to us immediately. We had private bodyguards, our own elevator in the hotel, an escape rope from our rooms, closed circuit television watching us, a motor van that wasn't allowed to stop, and rules that we never went in the same direction twice," he added.

Janet Haas won a silver medal in the Ninth Maccabiah Games tennis finals. "I have noticed when a Jewish athlete accomplishes a great feat, other Jews mention his accomplishments as well as his Jewishness in one sentence. I feel Jewish athletes should discuss Jewish issues with their Rabbi or other knowledgable Jews and then use their prominence to exert influence on public opinion. Like many black athletes, the Jewish athletes can contribute to influencing other Jews to act on matters—matters such as the Mid-East crisis," Haas said.

Another tennis star of the seventies, Brian Gottfried, disagreed with Janet Haas. "Sports and politics should be kept separate. The two have very little in common and it takes a different type of person to do each," Gottfried said.

A tendency to start slowly each season cast Richie Scheinblum in the shadow of Mike Epstein, Ron Blomberg, and other comparably gifted Jewish ballplayers. "I feel I have a Jewish following and I feel representative of a lot of people. When the 11 athletes were murdered in Munich, I felt it hit home; I wore the emblematic black band, which I felt was very important—not only because they were Jewish athletes, but because they were human beings," Scheinblum said. "I made some of my feelings known in print and did afterwards feel there would be a threatening response. But, nothing was said," he commented.

Marty Fleckman earned more recognition as an amateur golfer in the sixties than as a professional in the seventies. "The Munich tragedy is a definite threat to American Jewish athletes. I would be apprehensive to participate in many countries and I'm sure others would be also," he said.

Before his first major-league baseballgame, Mike Epstein had a worldwide Jewish following and the nickname, "Super Jew." The enormous publicity and extraordinary pressure apparently exerted too great a strain for him to realize his potential, although he did hit as many as 30 home runs in a season—a level he reached in 1969—and he led the 1972 World Champion Oakland A's in home runs with 26. During the previous decade, Jewish pitchers Howie Kitt and Mickey Abarbanel never advanced beyond the minor leagues after similar hype.

Not all Jewish athletes attracted such attention. During the early seventies, flame throwing right-hander Bob Grossman hurled two no-hitters for the University of Maryland to emerge quietly as selection number twenty-six in the Major League Baseball draft. Arm trouble prevented Grossman from advancing beyond the minor leagues. In the eighties, Temple University football quarterback Lee Saltz caught on in a reserve role in the National Football League without much fanfare. During the fifties and sixties, Jewish collegiate stars tended to draw more acclaim. Although he never made a professional basketball team, New York University's Barry Kramer attracted an enormous Jewish following as a high scoring forward during the sixties. The same could be said for Lenny Rosenbluth, of the University of North Carolina, for leading his team to victory in the NCAA tournament over Wilt Chamberlain's Kansas team during the fifties.

Mike "The Jewish Bomber" Rossman won the World Boxing Association Light Heavyweight Championship in 1978 with mobs of Jewish youths wearing yarmulkes in attendance. "There are many promoters asking for me. They are all out to make money as there isn't or hasn't been a good Jewish fighter for a long time," Rossman once said.

Nancy Ornstein depended on ground strokes and running away from the net to win the Middle Atlantic Women's Tennis Championship in 1974. "The Jewish athlete lucky enough to have influence should use it to our advantage. One time I played a German and felt as if it were German against Jew, rather than just a tennis match. It is hard to forget the past," Ornstein said.

Racing contender Steve Krisiloff's father voiced a different school of thought. "It's funny, but I don't recall anyone writing about Catholic athletes, or Protestant ones, or even Baptists. Mario Andretti is a Catholic, but I never see any mention of that fact when he wins a race. What is A. J. Foyt's religion, or the Unsers'?" Mike Krisiloff said. Another race car driver—one even better known than Steve Krisiloff—requested that this writer not mention his name for reasons connected with his personal security; and to avoid potential acts of terrorism by not publicizing the fact that he is Jewish. South African Jody Scheckter's religion became public knowledge several years later through his induction into a Jewish Sports Hall of Fame in Israel and subsequent inclusion in a compendium of biographies on Jewish athletes published in 1983.

Ironically, a gentile racing champion expressed enormous pride in his identification with Jewish issues. Shortly before Peter Revson's car crashed into flames in a training run, he said: "My mother is a WASP and I have been raised a Protestant. But, being half-Jewish, I am very sympathetic and understanding of Jewish problems. I have encountered very little prejudice on account of my ethnic background. If I do encounter it, I put myself in a position where I don't have to tolerate it."

Steve Greenberg followed his father's footsteps into professional baseball, but never lived up to the Hank Greenberg legend on the field. "My father was always proud of his heritage, but resented being called the greatest Jewish slugger of all time when in fact he may have been the greatest slugger of all time regardless of background," Steve Greenberg said. "It is important for people in the spotlight to be extremely careful when it comes to making public statements, because of the impact they have on millions of people. But, whenever an athlete—or anyone else—feels strongly about a political or social condition in the world, it should be his perogative to speak out and try to call attention to iniquities he perceives. I am glad that our hospitals, universities, and newspapers are crowded with Jewish doctors, professors, and writers. Who, after all, is going to benefit so much from a couple more Jewish pitchers and first basemen?" he added.

Pitcher Steve Stone followed the practice of many other Jewish athletes by combining scholarly pursuits with physical accomplishment. In 1980 Stone would burst into stardom by winning the American League Cy Young Award. "Any Jewish athlete scared away from professional sports either lacks the drive or the intestinal fortitude to make it anyway. We have a job to do and religion doesn't affect performance," Stone said.

Flamboyant outfielder Norm Miller, who roomed with pitcher Jim Bouton while Bouton was writing his bestseller, *Ball Four,* saw the Munich tragedy as a universal disaster, not just a blast on Jews. "My feelings and emotions were concern as a person—rather than as a Jew," Miller said. "Don't misunderstand me: it was just that I felt no matter what religious preference or nationality of the people involved, it was a universal disaster—not just a blast on Jews; as for it affecting me personally, I see no threat to myself or to future opportunities of Jews in sports," he added.

Heavyweight boxer Peter Brodsky reached the final round of the New Jersey Golden Gloves Boxing Championships the year 11 Israeli athletes died in Germany. He recalled with disgust how a Jewish manager promoted Adolf Hitler's sports hero, Max Schmeling to the Heavyweight Boxing Championship of the World during the Holocaust. "As far as Max Schmeling goes, I would like to beat his ass but good," Brodsky said. "If Jewish athletes would join together to motivate other Jews to actively engage in athletics, maybe enough prominent Jewish athletes could enlighten some people about the various tragedies that have befallen Jewish people," he added.

In the Washington, D.C. area and throughout the nation, the Jewish Athletic and Cultural Associations have surfaced to increase Jewish participation in Jewish activities, foster Jewish pride and self-confidence, and offer training in self-defense. President Steven Eisman stated, "As long as the athlete is engaged in the right sport and performs as well as a Sandy Koufax, all is well. But, the American Jew was embarrased by Mike Epstein's poor performance in the 1972 World Series. We live in an age of ethnicity. Timing, opportunity, fear of retribution, and economic possibilities can stifle one's participation in activism," Eisman said. "Don't expect a Mark Spitz to reject seven gold medals when the Israeli team is wasted by terrorists; but, John Carlos felt so strongly about the degradation of blacks in 1968, he set himself up to be ejected from Olympic competition," he said.

The Jewish sports executive has also played a major role in merging the public's association of Jewish people with athletics. As The Clown Prince of Baseball, Al Schacht created good will for world Jewry for more than 50 years with a comedy act. "In all, I entertained in 25 different World Series and 15 All-Star games," Schacht said.

In the decade between 1956 to 1966, the Boston Celtics won nine basketball world championships—eight of them in succession and all under the coaching of Arnold "Red" Auerbach. "I feel that most of the American Jews take pride in the Jewish athletes and their accomplishments because I hear these comments wherever I go," Auerbach said.

Co-owner and general manager of professional basketball and football championship teams in Minnesota, Max Winter had once built a reputation for himself in sports as a gymnast and ice skater in Austria. "As for Jewish athletes using their recognition to benefit their fellow Jews, I do believe that Mr. Spitz had a great opportunity to assert himself on many issues that would have been published around the world," Winter said. "As for naming the greatest Jewish quarterback, it would be unfair for me to rank Sid Luckman, Benny Friedman, and Harry Newman even though I was fortunate to see them all on several occasions. All three of them were very great quarterbacks and, perhaps given the same chance on the same teams, I doubt that there could be a great difference," he said.

Professional basketball and hockey teams owner Abe Pollin launched a drive to build a memorial at Tel Aviv University for the Israeli athletes slain at the Munich Olympics in 1972. "As an American, a Jew, a person involved with sports, and most of all as a human being: I felt the memorial was the most effective thing I could do. This was my way of protest. I think it is incumbent on every Jew to recognize when an injustice against humanity has taken place and to enlighten others about that injustice," Pollin continued. "When that injustice affects only Jews: the burden of informing the rest of the world rests upon the Jewish voice," he said.

President of the National Football League in the late sixties—during the time the sport passed baseball as the country's most popular spectator team sport—and owner of the Cleveland Browns, Art Modell proved himself to be a sensitive human being in 1962. His new prize acquisition Ernie Davis—already considered a runningback of the Jimmy Brown caliber although just out of college—had acute monocytic leukemia. It was only a matter of time. *Cleveland Plain Dealer*'s Chuck Heaton, then a beat reporter, covered the Ernie Davis affair. "Model asked us not to publicize the nature of the illness because David had not been informed. Before the announcement of the nature of the disease some months later, Ernie had been informed. I believe he felt so well at the time that he believed he might lick it," Heaton said. When asked about the relative scarcity of Jewish athletes, Modell said: "I guess that the reason there are not so many professional Jewish athletes stems from the fact that our parents from the time we were very young tried to direct us in the careers of law, medicine, and other similar professions."

World Boxing Association Commissioner Abe J. Greene imposed a ban on religious credal symbols in the ring. "When the late Abe Simon—mastodonic heavyweight—was preparing to appear in a New Jersey ring, he wore a Jewish star on the right side of his shorts. I took him aside and directed him to get other tights or turn his own inside out. Simon demurred, insisting he was proud of his race. I told him that he was not boxing as a Jew and that this went for all credoes. Simon insisted on his right to wear the symbol, whereupon I opened my shirt and pointed to my own prayer

(Photo courtesy of The Jewish Athletic and Cultural Association)

STEVE EISMAN

shawl. I told Simon I had worn the prayer shawl constantly since boyhood, but not on display. Simon got the point and never again wore the Mogen David," Green said.

As president and controlling owner of baseball's Baltimore Orioles, Jerry Hoffberger said: "After the Munich tragedy, I did not do anything differently and I did not fear that the terrorism would have any effect on the performance of top-notch Jewish players such as Kenny Holtzman or Richie Scheinblum."

Carroll Rosenbloom built football dynasties on the east and west coasts. "Most Jewish athletes perform a valuable public relations service for American Jews. Certainly, Sandy Koufax did because of his great talent, intelligence, modesty, courage, and exemplary behavior," Rosenbloom said.

Gabe Paul built a reputation as one of Major League Baseball's shrewdest traders. "I don't feel that an athlete feels prejudice as much as any normal person, because in athletics: it is the ability that counts," Paul noted.

The show business expertise of Sonny Werblin helped his team's American Football League promote a merger with the established National Football League. "As an American, I think there is too much polarization in this country as it is," Werblin said, refusing to comment further.

Former National Basketball Association head coach Roy Rubin disagreed: "There are so few Jews participating in professional sports that a Jewish player or coach provides incentives for those of his race who are so inspired."

Former basketball executive Arnold A. Heft once had a promising baseball career as a pitcher. "Unlike today, Jewish athletes didn't always receive the recognition we merited. I won 22 games in the high minors one year and hardly anyone noticed; other athletes were wined and dined. I served in World War II not just because of the holocaust of Jews in Germany, but because I am an American. Hank Greenberg did serve the five peak years of his career in heavy combat. But, so did Ted Williams, who wasn't Jewish," Heft said.

Former National Football League team owner Jerry Wolman earned his financial fortune from scratch. "I have the faith from my religion that if you do what is right, you will have peace of mind. It is the responsibility of all people to stand up and act as spokesmen for what they believe is true," he said.

Now, media commentators expect a proportionate amount of Jewish participation in American sports. The most famous fight announcer in history, Sam Taub, covered more than 7,500 boxing and 1,000 wrestling matches. "You can find a history of Jews in boxing, baseball, and football. We have had some great Jewish players in basketball and even hockey. We also have quite a representation in soccer," Taub said.

Newspaper columnist and television commentator Morrie Siegel called Rocky Marciano's knockout of Jersey Joe Walcott the greatest of ethnic sports victories. Siegel said, "The ring was deluged with Italian kids. And, I think black athletes are more conscious of their blackness than Jewish athletes are of their Jewishness. I would like to see Jewish athletes speak out on Jewish issues the way black athletes do on black issues."

From the Brooklyn Dodgers baseball team to the New York City Off Track Betting Corporation, Irving Rudd has held numerous sports publicity positions. "I guess my proudest accomplishment was being the one person responsible for bringing from the Soviet Union the first harness horses ever to compete on American soil in 1963. I made known my feelings regarding the treatment of Soviet Jews. I made it a point to visit synagogues wherever I went and saw to it that my Jewish brethren were well supplied with *siddurim* and *talithim*," Rudd said.

One-time president of the New York Baseball Writers Association and the public relations director of the American Basketball League New York Nets, Barney Kremenko cited Benny Leonard, for special accolade, "Leonard was suave, debonair, extremely clever, and a good puncher as well. He had patent leather hair always neatly combed; the legend about him was that you were in your greatest trouble when you ruffled his hair. His boxing style set a pattern."

Calvin R. Griffith, president of baseball's Minnesota Twins, summed up the feelings of most gentile sports executives. "The incident in Munich may have made our Jewish athletes try even harder to excel in their field," Griffith said.

The Fellowship of Christian Athletes has exerted tremendous influence and extraordinary public relations for Christian people, much to the credit of communications director Gary Warner. "We are the Fellowship of Christian Athletes, because to us who are Christian men it is the Christian and not the Fellowship or Athletes words that are the heart of our program. If people remember great accomplishments coming from Christian athletes and not Jewish athletes, why not start a Fellowship of Jewish Athletes?" Ward asked.

It is true: Jewish athletes are no longer considered a departure from the regular assortment of Jewish people. Former Israeli Ambassador to the United States Simcha Dinitz agreed. "The Jewish image doesn't need improvement, but participation in sports helps maintain it," Dinitz added.

The question regarding whether a famous Jewish person outside of politics assumes an appropriate role when publicly taking a political stance that would have magnified ramifications on issues of interest to all Jewish people has been overtaken by events—events such as a seemingly unified media in 1988 giving instant celebrity status to any moderately prominent American Jew speaking out against Israel for her forcefully resilient stand against violent Palestinians protesting Zionism and reluctance to relinquish land for temporary peace; or negotiate with terrorist organizations who refuse to recognize the legitimacy of her existence.

Around midnight of March 11, 1988, movie actor Richard Dreyfuss—who was still in the process of attempting to rebuild a reputation shattered by a highly publicized arrest for cocaine—appeared with lesser known Leon Wieseltier, Literary Editor of the *New Republic,* and with Israeli United Nations Ambassador Benjamin Netanyahu, against the questioning of moderator Ted Koppel on *Nightline.* The teaming of two American Jewish opponents against one Israeli in support of Israeli policies cast a distorted impression that they both reflected the balance of opinions on the subject by American Jews primarily because of the implied importance given to their statements by Ted Koppel.

Right then, a famous Jewish athlete—even one unheard of for years—could have wiped out that artificially distorted impression with statements in support of Israel either by having created a vocal enough response on the subject to have forced an invitation to appear on the show or by publicly responding to it the following day. It is at times such as then—when it is unpopular or unprofitable to appear supportive of Jewish interests—when a prominent Jewish voice is most needed.

The March 15, 1988 *USA Today* cover story cited Dreyfuss's appearance on *Nightline* and an earlier letter with the same sentiment in *The New York Times* op-ed page under the by-line of actor Woody Allen, as implied evidence that American Jews were "anguishing" over their support of Israel. Even a moderately famous Jewish athlete has the potential to command national attention in a political arena, as demonstrated by Richard Dreyfuss and Leon Wieseltier, but not the obligation. The question regarding whether a famous Jewish athlete should use that prominence to exert influence on public opinion in support of Jewish interests is a personal choice.

But, only the voices from prominent Jewish persons, such as famous actors, athletes, politicians, etc., can demand sufficient exposure to combat apparent attempts to slant public opinion against Jewish interests.

In addition to counteracting rebellious sentiments of individuals against traditionally unified Jewish positions that reflect the collective opinion of American Jewry supporting Zionism, a famous Jewish person—whether an actor, athlete, or distinguished in another field—may say the things that need to be said that representatives of a tax exempt Jewish organization cannot. When Jewish organizations release statements simply expressing disappointment over—say—the Vatican's amazingly post-Holocaust guiltless refusal to recognize Israel's right to exist or the Pope's meeting with the terrorist Yasser Arafat, only a famous Jewish person has a platform from which to effectively respond. When isolated individuals of Jewish heritage band together and call themselves Jews for Jesus, only a Jewish person with celebrity status has the media exposure required in making it clear to the public that by virtue of their stated beliefs these people are not Jews and their actions do not represent Jewish people. Various Jewish groups could risk losing their charitable status by condemning a political candidate, even when isolated Jewish individuals with questionable intent attempt to convey an erroneous impression of widespread support for the candidate among Jews and the candidate is as diametrically opposed to Jewish interests, such as a Jesse Helms or Jesse Jackson.

Even the Jewish athlete who wishes to keep his personal opinions private must recognize that silence sometimes conveys an unintended signal of approval or at least apathy, when in fact the opposite might be true. With actors such as Woody Allen and Richard Dreyfuss garnering headlines by exercising their legitimate right to express opinions that may conflict with traditional Jewish positions, the burden falls upon other famous Jews to speak out if they disagree.

THE JEWISH-AMERICAN ALL-TIME ATHLETIC RANKINGS

The Jewish Magnificent Seven

1. Hank Greenberg
2. Sid Luckman
3. Benny Leonard
4. Sandy Koufax
5. Dolph Schayes
6. Ron Mix
7. Ken Holtzman

HANK GREENBERG

HANK GREENBERG

In April 1973, when I originally set out to establish this Jewish Sports Hall of Fame and All-Time Athletic Rankings, I turned to historians for help in comparing the then current and recent crop of Jewish athletes with those who had performed before I was born. I had just turned 24. As an enclosure of a letter to me dated May 23, 1973, from John Redding, Librarian of the National Baseball Hall of Fame and Museum, I received a September 12, 1935 *Sporting News* article proclaiming Hank Greenberg "the greatest Jewish ballplayer of all time." The reporter, Frederick G. Lieb, wrote that he had been following Lou Gehrig as a schoolboy athlete but first heard of Hank Greenberg, then also a schoolboy in New York, from Detroit baseball writer Harry Bullion. It was then that Bullion told Lieb: "We have a high school kid from New York with us that hits a ball farther than any kid I ever saw. The distance he can get is amazing. His name is Hank Greenberg."

To appreciate the awesome power that Hank Greenberg generated in hitting a baseball, simply understand that he was a better home-run hitter than Hank Aaron—the man who would topple the legendary Babe Ruth's all-time mark 26 years after Greenberg retired. Compare their records. In addition to missing virtually an entire season of his prime with a broken wrist, Greenberg lost nearly five years—five years at his absolute peak—to World War II combat service during the Holocaust. Still, he retired with 331 home runs in 5,193 at bats—a ratio of one home run every 15.69 times at bat. Aaron hit his record-breaking 715th home run in at-bat number 11,288—a ratio of a home run every 15.79 times at bat. During the three years preceding Greenberg's military service, he averaged 44 home runs in 543 at bats—a one out of 12.34 at-bat home-run ratio, which if added to his actual statistics to impute what his record might have been over the five peak years he missed would suggest that Greenberg would have retired with a 14.35 ratio from 551 home runs in 7,908 at bats. Now, consider that Aaron played his home games in two of the easiest home-run ballparks—Milwaukee and Atlanta, especially Atlanta where previously ordinary players like former infielder Davey Johnson blossomed into 40-plus homer per year slugger. To demonstrate this Aaron advantage, simply compare the 201.5 average derived from 196 home runs hit in Milwaukee during 1965, Aaron's last year as a Brave there, and the 207 home runs hit during Aaron's first year at Atlanta in 1966 to the 170.5 average number of home runs hit those years at Detroit where Greenberg had earlier played—an 18 percent advantage. Dividing the imputed 14.35 Greenberg home-run ratio into the 11,288 number of at bats Aaron needed for his record and multiplying that quotient by 1.18 to account for the differences in ballparks, yields a projected Hank Greenberg career home run total of 928—a number that would never have been equaled.

Hank Greenberg reflected upon his career and his reaction to the 1972 murder of Israeli athletes at Munich in a letter to me dated June 5, 1973. First, I had asked him about prejudice. For example, the 1935 *Sporting News* article fell under a banner headline that read: "Oi, Oi, Oh, Boy! Hail That Long-Sought Hebrew Star." Boxed in with a cartoon of Greenberg was a caricature of a circular pacing and large-nosed man hunched over with these words of wisdom attributed to him: "Oy Yoy-Oy Yoy." In response to my question, Greenberg responded: "During my baseball career, I do not recall experiencing any prejudice; I do not consider name calling racial prejudice."

Turning to the Munich murders, Greenberg wrote: "Like all civilized people, I was shocked by the tragedy at Munich. Senseless killing is difficult to understand and particularly regrettable when it takes place during a sporting event. Sportsmanship and good fellowship are what the Olympic Games are supposed to be about."

Then, I raised the sensitive question regarding whether the Munich murders posed a threat in his mind to American Jewish athletes such as his son Steve, who was playing minor league baseball at the time. "My son Steve has no fear participating in athletics, nor do I have any for him," he responded. Then, he added: "in this current world atmosphere—where tragic events take place daily—one must continue to live as though these happenings do not take place."

To get an even closer look at the greatest Jewish athlete, Hank Greenberg, I turned to his son Steve. The younger Greenberg had made a name for himself at Yale University as first baseman and captain of the baseball team—positions once held by George Bush—and goalie of the soccer team, where the spectacular save enabled him to repeat his selection as a junior on the All-Ivy and All-New England teams and also earned him a place on the Coaches' All-America Second Team.

In a letter to me dated June 11, 1973, Steve Greenberg elaborated on his father's letter. "I am aware of a particular interest in my career by Jewish fans, especially so because my father is remembered by most of them," Steve Greenberg wrote. "Of course in places like Pittsfield, Massachusetts and Burlington, North Carolina, there are not a great many Jews to begin with," he added. "In Spokane and Denver, however, I am always aware of a special following, which I honestly enjoy. That my career is of interest to Jewish fans pleases me," he went on to write; adding: "I always try to accept speaking invitations at local Jewish Community Centers."

Steve Greenberg then reflected upon his father: "I don't particularly understand the relevance of the term "Jewish Hope." Naturally, some people will always associate my name with my being Jewish; but, I think every athlete should be evaluated on his athletic ability and not his heredity. My father was always proud of his heritage, but resented being called the greatest Jewish slugger of all time when in fact he may have been the greatest slugger of all time regardless of background. It would be equally meaningless to call Hank Aaron the greatest Negro slugger. Why confine a man's athletic ability to his racial or religious background? Statistics and records are not subdivided along those lines in any sport. Every athlete wants to be judged and accepted along with all other players—not just Jewish, or Black, or Puerto Rican players."

I asked Steve Greenberg to discuss how he perceived the participation in major league baseball at that time by several other Jewish athletes affected his desire to follow in his father's footsteps. "I am pleased guys like Ken Holtzman, Mike Epstein, Richie Scheinblum, and Ron Blomberg have achieved success in the major leagues. But, I have never felt that their careers have any effect or real direct relationship to mine. My father's career really has no bearing on mine. I do feel a kind of closeness to other Jewish ballplayers that is difficult to explain, since Blomberg and Epstein are the only other Jewish players I know. I follow Holtzman and the others with interest," he responded.

I asked Steve Greenberg if the attainment of fame carries with it an obligation to exert influence in support of issues concerning the ethnic group with which the public associates a particular individual when that individual is devoted to the interests of his group. This was his reply: "As far as speaking out on critical issues is concerned, I believe that anyone—regardless of his job or influence—should be able to speak out.

Unfortunately, it often appears that people only listen to so-called celebrities whether they be politicians, athletes, or movie stars. It is important for these people in the spotlight to be extremely careful when it comes to making public statements, because of the impact they have on millions of people. But, whenever an athlete—or anyone else—feels strongly about a political or social condition in the world, it should be his prerogative to speak out and try to call attention to iniquities he perceives."

Next, Steve Greenberg focused on the threat of terrorism. "Just living in the world today is a threat to one's personal well-being, regardless of race or creed," he wrote. "Thousands of Southeast Asians found this out," he added. Then he turned to the Munich murders with this observation: "The Munich tragedy merely confirmed this fact. There is no telling where or when human beings will slaughter other human beings in the name of nationalism or patriotism. Human slaughter is not confined to Jews, although we have certainly known more than our share of persecution and senseless butchery."

Steve Greenberg saw no implications threatening his own well-being from the Munich murders: "I try not to consider the myriad ways in which my well-being is threatened daily as result of our polarized civilization. Any threat to my existence is neither greater nor smaller than the threat hanging over the head of every other human being from the rice paddies of Cambodia to the streets of any American city to the precarious *kibbutzim* beneath the Golan Heights."

Finally, Steve Greenberg reflected upon himself: "To think that by being a baseball player I am somehow exalted among other men is a vain thought. Ballplayers are no better or worse than people anywhere else. We merely attract more attention. And Jews will continue to play baseball wherever they have a combination of the ability and desire to do so. It is usually the latter that is lacking."

Then, he added: "I am glad that our hospitals, universities, and newspapers are crowded with Jewish doctors, professors, and writers. Who, after all, is going to benefit so much from a couple more Jewish pitchers and first basemen?"

That display of modesty by Steve Greenberg sounds much like his father, when the senior Greenberg would refuse to discount accomplishments of current players on the premise that a more lively ball, diluted pitching talent because of expansion, smaller ballparks, more games in a season, and better conditioning opportunities have made it easier to hit home runs. In fact, Hank Greenberg took enormous pride in Roger Maris' successful chase of Babe Ruth's single season home run record. It was Hank Greenberg who brought Maris into baseball during Greenberg's days as general manager of the Cleveland Indians. Until Maris' 163-game chase of Ruth's 1927 record of 60 home runs set in a 154-game season culminated with home run number 61 in 1961, Hank Greenberg had come the closest to breaking the record. In 1938, Hank Greenberg slugged home run number 58 in team game number 150. Like Maris' Yankees in 1961, Greenberg's 1938 Tigers had been involved in a tie game—which, in effect, added a game to the team schedule when it was replayed. In 1927, Ruth had hit home run number 58 in team game number 153—one team game after Roger Maris would do it 34 years later. With five games to play, Hank Greenberg stood on the verge of accomplishing the impossible. Whether Hank Greenberg's failure to hit another home run that season could be attributed to a conspiracy by pitchers to keep the baseball out of the strike zone, as one former player of that era suggested to me, is purely a matter of conjecture. But, if such a conspiracy did exist, Hank Greenberg would have been forced to swing at bad pitches—which would have been a disadvantage unprecedented in major league baseball. It was in the last game of that 1938 season when Greenberg uttered what would become a famous concession line, much like boxer Jack Dempsey's "Honey, I forgot to duck" quip that Ronald Reagan recited on his way to surgery after being shot. When darkness forced umpire George Moriarty to call a premature end in the sixth inning, he said to Greenberg: "Sorry, Hank; but this is as far as I can go." Then Greenberg uttered the famous line: "That's all right, George, this is as far as I can go, too."

Greenberg's 63 doubles in 1934, his astronomical 183 runs batted in during 1937 and 170 runs batted in during 1935, 58 home runs in 1938, and a batting average rarely below .320 demonstrate that it is he and not the legendary great Lou Gehrig who belongs at first base on any mythical all-time team compilations. Because Hank Greenberg traded the prime of his career for combat fatigues, few people recognize that he was actually better than Gehrig. The year he returned from combat, after nearly five years away, Greenberg hit the most dramatic grand slam home run in baseball history; in the ninth inning of the last game of the season and the bases loaded, Hank Greenberg won the American League pennant for the Detroit Tigers with a shot heard on radios around the world.

If Hank Greenberg were alive today, he—like anyone, but magnified many times because of who he was and what only he could do—would undoubtedly take a page from The Twilight Zone and go back into time to do things differently with the benefit of hindsight. One can only postulate what a difference in history and particularly Jewish history there might be.

First, it is hard to believe that Greenberg would have signed with the Detroit Tigers if he knew in advance that he would be good enough to play wherever he wanted. The friendly confines of the incredibly close-in left field wall at Boston's Fenway Park might have posed a target that could have attracted 60 to 70 home runs a season from the pull hitting right-handed Greenberg. But, the deafening roar of an enormous Jewish following that would later emerge in New York would have kept Hank Greenberg at his Bronx hometown with the Yankees. If he could have foreseen the future, Greenberg might have attempted to use that Jewish following in attempting to change the course of the world.

In May 1939, Hank Greenberg was fresh into his first season after captivating the world's attention with his nearly successful pursuit of Babe Ruth's single season home run record. Hank Greenberg was a bigger than life hero. Meanwhile, a ship sailed out of Germany with 930 Jews given the last opportunity to escape the torture, rape, and murder that would befall six million Jews under German control in what would eventually become known simply as The Holocaust. By refusing their entry into the United States on the bureaucratic excuse of a so-called quota system in effect at the time, President Franklin Delano Roosevelt directed the desperate Jews back into the hands of the German murderers led by Adolf Hitler. After a well-received speech at the American University in 1976, the controversial Rabbi Meir Kahane—founder of the Jewish Defense League—told me: "The public misplaced trust in Franklin Delano Roosevelt, so his anti-Semitism cost Jewish Lives. Our martyrs needed someone who could have said 'Bomb Auschwitz' loud enough for newspapers to print." Unlike attorney Louis Marshall, who brought anti-Semite Henry Ford to his knees by mobilizing a successful boycott of his cars in the twenties, Rabbi Kahane confronted a comfortable post-Holocaust American Jewry unmotivated to collectively receive his accurately foreboding message. He would later win elected office in Israel with a controversial hard-line platform.

Roosevelt turned a deaf ear to the respectful pleas of Jewish leaders. But, if Hank Greenberg had known—as it was later found that Roosevelt had—what stood to happen to those 930 Jews and the millions more who followed; if he could have foreseen the success of leader-directed civil disobedience by Jews for the benefit of black Americans three decades later that created the only opportunity for Dr. Martin Luther King Jr. to eventually assume a leadership role himself; and if he had been playing in New York where there were enough Jewish people to unite in sufficient mass behind a charismatic leader; Hank Greenberg might have found himself directing a chanting of "No more quotas FDR . . ." But, he didn't; he couldn't; and he wasn't. An understanding then of what the word Holocaust means might have kept Hank Greenberg at home in the spotlight exerting pressure through the public to "Bomb the crematorium at Auschwitz." Perhaps a hero of the magnitude of a Hank Greenberg could have made a difference. When Israeli athletes were murdered in Munich in 1972, perhaps that chance of possibly making a difference is the underlying motive that prompted then baseball superstar Ken Holtzman to risk marking himself for another terrorist act by wearing a black armband around his uniform while playing . If Hank Greenberg was still playing then, no doubt he probably would have done the same.

Even 23 years after his retirement, Hank Greenberg still had to endure subtle reminders of constant awareness by journalists of his being Jewish. In a *Sporting News* article dated October 3, 1970, under the by-line of Bob Broeg, Greenberg was reported as having been subjected to razzing from members of the St. Louis Cardinals Gashouse Gang after his temporary demotion from fourth to sixth in the batting order before the fourth game of the 1934 World Series. "The Jews long since have proved that, even if they don't like it, they can take it," Broeg reported. "Greenberg came out in the fourth game with a record-tying four hits, including two doubles," he added. It was in the final stages of the pennant race leading to that world series when Greenberg made banner headlines by sitting out a critical game that the Tigers went on to lose because it fell on Yom Kippur.

Although Greenberg retired in 1947 and a former player becomes eligible for induction after only five years out of the game, it was not until 1956 when he received the required number of votes to become the first Jewish person to gain entrance into the National Baseball Hall of Fame. His plaque reads: "ONE OF BASEBALL'S GREATEST RIGHT-HANDED BATTERS. TIED FOR MOST HOME RUNS BY RIGHT-HANDED BATTER IN 1938, 58. MOST RUNS-BATTED-IN 1935–37–40–46, AND HOME RUNS 1938–40–46. WON 1945 PENNANT WITH GRAND SLAM HOME RUN IN 9TH INNING. PLAYED IN 4 WORLD SERIES, 2 ALL-STAR GAMES. MOST VALUABLE A.L. PLAYER TWICE, 1935–1940. LIFETIME BATTING AVERAGE .313."

Still the question persists regarding just how many baseball records would have been irrevocably broken had Hank Greenberg—who would go on to become America's first $100,000-a-year salaried athlete—not given up the five prime years of his career. As a full colonel on General Douglas MacArthur's immediate staff during the war, my father—Abraham G. (Al) Silverman—played handball with Hank Greenberg and talked with Greenberg in-depth. In the letter I received from Hank Greenberg in 1973 while researching this book, he recalled their friendship. My father once explained, "Getting to know Hank as I did convinced me that he had an internal resolution to stay in the service, even though it meant foregoing enormous earnings and, of course, risking his life."

Although—according to the October 3, 1970 *Sporting News*—a Florida doctor declared Greenberg unfit for military duty because of flat feet, "Hitler and his purge were in the offing and before long Hank, of Jewish faith, was in the service as a private . . . on maneuvers in the swampy southland." Although the law permitted discharge of men who were 28 or older, the 30-year-old Greenberg entered officer training for more combat. At 34, Captain Greenberg returned to baseball with four battle stars and a home run. The following season, Greenberg slugged 44 homers only to hear on radio during the off season that he had been waived out of the league to the Pittsburg Pirates where he became the first $100,000-player to close out his unparalleled career. At that time, it would have been fitting to again say—for the last time—"That's all right, George, this is as far as I can go too."

Text of Letter From Hank Greenberg to This Author, Dated June 5, 1973

"During my baseball career, I do not recall experiencing any prejudice; I do not consider name calling racial prejudice.

"Like all civilized people, I was shocked by the tragedy at Munich. Senseless killing is difficult to understand and particularly regrettable when it takes place during a sporting event. Sportsmanship and good fellowship are what the Olympic Games are supposed to be about.

"My son Steve has no fear participating in athletics, nor do I have any for him. In this current world atmosphere—where tragic events take place daily—one must continue to live as though these happenings do not take place.

"I keep busy with my involvements in personal investments. I have no connections with baseball; but, I take an interest in the game as any Jew and doubly so because of Steve's involvement. My best personal regards to your father."

Text of Letter From Steve Greenberg to This Author, Dated June 11, 1973

"I am aware of a particular interest in my career by Jewish fans, especially so because my father is remembered by most of them. Of course in places like Pittsfield, Massachusetts, and Burlington, North Carolina, there are not a great many Jews to begin with. In Spokane and Denver, however, I am always aware of a special following, which I honestly enjoy. That my career is of interest to Jewish fans pleases me. I always try to accept speaking invitations at local Jewish Community Centers.

"I don't particularly understand the relevance of the term 'Jewish Hope.' Naturally, some people will always associate my name with my being Jewish; but, I think every athlete should be evaluated on his athletic ability and not his heredity. My father was always proud of his heritage, but resented being called the greatest Jewish slugger of all time when in fact he may have been the greatest slugger of all time regardless of background. It would be equally meaningless to call Hank Aaron the greatest Negro slugger. Why confine a man's athletic ability to his racial or religious background? Statistics and records are not subdivided along these lines in any sport. Every athlete wants to be judged and accepted along with all other players—not just Jewish, or Black or Puerto Rican players."

"I am pleased guys like Ken Holtzman, Mike Epstein, Richie Scheinblum and Ron Blomberg have achieved success in the Major Leagues. But, I have never felt that their careers have any effect or real direct relationship to mine. My father's career really has no bearing on mine. I do feel a kind of closeness to other Jewish ballplayers that is difficult to explain, since Blomberg and Epstein are the only other Jewish players I know. I follow Holtzman and the others with interest.

"As far as speaking out on critical issues is concerned, I believe that anyone—regardless of his job or influence—should be able to speak out. Unfortunately, it often appears that people only listen to so-called celebrities whether they be politicians, athletes or movie stars. It is important for these people in the spotlight to be extremely careful when it comes to making public statements, because of the impact they have on millions of people. But, whenever an athlete—or anyone else—feels strongly about a political or social position in the world, it should be his perogative to speak out and try to call attention to iniquities he perceives."

"Just living in the world today is a threat to one's personal well-being, regardless of race or creed. Thousands of Southeast Asians found this out. The Munich tragedy merely confirmed this fact. There is no telling where or when human beings will slaughter other human beings in the name of nationalism or patriotism. Human slaughter is not confined to Jews, although we have certainly known more than our share or persecution and senseless butchery.

"I try not to consider the myriad ways in which my well-being is threatened daily as result of our polarized civilization. Any threat to my existence is neither greater nor smaller than the threat hanging over the head of every other human being from the rice paddies of Cambodia to the streets of any American city to the precarious *kibbutzim* beneath the Golan Heights.

"To think that by being a baseball player I am somehow exalted among other men is a vain thought. Ballplayers are no better or worse than people anywhere else. We merely attract more attention. And Jews will continue to play baseball wherever they have a combination of the ability and the desire to do so. It is usually the latter that is lacking.

"I am glad that our hospitals, universities and newspapers are crowded with Jewish doctors, professors and writers. Who, after all, is going to benefit so much from a couple more Jewish pitchers and first basemen?"

Hank Greenberg's Home Run Chase
Hank Greenberg's Career Record

Settling on Hank Greeberg as the number one ranked Jewish athlete of all time—the greatest Jewish athlete ever—came after exhaustive documentation, systematic consultation, and inevitable deliberation that included reflection upon a claim baseball's legendary Ted Williams frequently made. Williams claimed that hitting a baseball was the single most difficult athletic accomplishment. With a speed often in excess of 90 miles per hour and sudden changes of direction, a pitched ball carries the ever-present threat of brutal mortality to a batter armed only with a thin wooden bat and only an instant to locate the resultantly small white blur before even attempt to make contact with it. By achieving indisputably elite distinction at the most difficult physical endeavor in sports, Hank Greenberg is indeed number one.

HANK GREENBERG'S HOMERUN CHASE

Homerun Number	Team Game for Babe Ruth in 1927	Team Game for Hank Greenberg in 1938	Homerun Number	Team Game for Babe Ruth in 1927	Team Game for Hank Greenberg in 1938
1	4	1	31	94	87
2	11	3	32	95	88
3	12	7	33	95	88
4	14	14	34	98	90
5	16	16	35	106	90
6	16	18	36	110	91
7	24	20	37	114	92
8	25	25	38	115	99
9	29	30	39	118	109
10	33	30	40	120	109
11	34	32	41	124	110
12	37	35	42	125	112
13	39	37	43	127	114
14	41	50	44	128	119
15	42	54	45	132	120
16	43	55	46	132	122
17	47	59	47	133	132
18	48	60	48	134	133
19	52	61	49	134	133
20	52	61	50	138	135
21	53	65	51	139	139
22	55	66	52	140	140
23	60	72	53	143	140
24	60	74	54	147	143
25	70	74	55	148	146
26	73	75	56	149	146
27	78	80	57	152	150
28	79	81	58	153	150
29	79	85	59	153	
30	83	87	60	154	

HANK GREENBERG'S CAREER RECORD

Teams	Positions	At bats	Hits	Doubles	HRs	RBIs	Batting Average
Detroit 1933-41 1945-46 Pittsburgh 1947	First Base and Out- field	5193	1628	379	331	1276	.313
HANK GREENBERG'S CAREER HIGHS:			203	63	58	183	.340

HANK GREENBERG'S BEST FIVE YEARS

1934		593	201	63	26	139	.339
1935		619	203	46	36	170	.328
1937		594	200	49	40	183	.337
1938		556	175	23	58	146	.315
1940		573	195	50	41	150	.340
Composite		587	195	46	40	158	.332

Awesome championship game performances, introduction of the T formation, and the spectacular touchdown pass after defense and special team play made Sid Luckman the greatest quarterback in the history of professional football. (Photo courtesy of the Chicago Bears)

SID LUCKMAN

Before attempting to compare passing records of a Johnny Unitas or Sonny Jurgenson era quarterback with the performance of Sid Luckman in the forties, imagine Unitas or Jurgenson staying on the field to intercept passes on defense and to punt on special teams. Remember that Joe Namath compiled most of his statistics in a then defensively lean American Football League; and that the touchdown passes of the John Elway and Dan Marino era came after rule changes restricting the amount of interference that can be applied to eligible receivers. Sid Luckman is the greatest one of them all—the greatest quarterback ever to play the game.

In a May 18, 1973 letter to me from Pro Football's Hall of Fame Librarian Jim Campbell, responding to my initiation then of a proposed book establishing a Jewish Sports Hall of Fame, I received evidence supporting a convincing argument that Sid Luckman's accomplishments will never be equaled in the modern age of specialists. Campbell provided an insight of Luckman's punting, defensive play, and rushing in addition to his performance as quarterback.

Regarding Sid Luckman as a punter, Campbell wrote: "Luckman also punted 156 times for the Bears during his career. His punting average for his whole career is not available, but his best single-season mark was 41.0 yards for 13 punts in 1941. The most he punted in any one season was 34 times for a 35.9-yard average in 1943."

The most remarkable extracurricular activity cited by Campbell was Luckman's defensive play. "Early in his career, he also played a lot on defense and he shows 14 interceptions for 293 yards and one touchdown . . ." Campbell wrote, adding: "He intercepted three passes for 52 yards in 1941, four for 96 yards and one touchdown in 1942, four for 85 yards in 1943, two for 36 in 1944, and one for 24 in 1946."

Campbell also focused on Sid Luckman's rushing record: "He is listed with 180 rushes during his career, obviously, many of them came when he was tackled trying to pass with statistics being recorded differently in those days. His most productive rushing season was in 1947 when he had 10 carries for 86 yards."

The Chicago Bears' 1946 *Press Book* provides the most explicit insight of Luckman's passing reputation: "Most football men rate Sid Luckman and Sammy Baugh as the two greatest forward passers of all-time . . . (but) there are coaches like Greasy Neale who contend that Luckman is the peer of them all as a passer . . . he may throw less aerials (than Baugh), and as a result complete a few less. But in the matter of touchdown passes and yardage gained by passes, Luckman is tops by himself. George Halas . . . likes to talk about Sid Luckman, 'Mister Quarterback,'" . . . (as) the greatest quarterback ever to work the T (formation) . . . Halas, and there are others too, insists that Sid is the slickest ball handler and smartest signal caller in the history of the T formation."

The 1952 edition of the *Official National Football League Encyclopedia* had this to say about the legendary Jewish quarterback: "Sid Luckman gets a unanimous rating as the smartest field general football has ever known. His teammates and opponents both attest that he won more games with his head than most teams do with their muscles. He was an excellent open-field runner, a top-flight passer, an adequate punter, also an accurate extra-point man—although he seldom performed as such."

After lettering three years both as a halfback in football and shortstop in baseball, Sid Luckman joined the Chicago Bears in 1939 after the Pittsburgh Steelers had traded their draft rights in the first round to Chicago. Luckman became the first exponent of the T-formation after being shifted to quarterback the following season. He led the Bears to four straight National Football League then Western Division Championships in 1940 through 1943 and another in 1946 with a World Championship in every one of those years except 1942, when the Washington Redskins rebounded from a 1940 Luckman directed 73–0 trouncing to post a 14–6 win. He was All-National Football League quarterback seven straight seasons and Most Valuable Player in 1943, when he passed for 28 touchdowns in a season that was approximately half as long as those expanded through modern scheduling. Sid Luckman retired in 1950. He surfaced again in 1965 to become the first Jewish player inducted into the Pro Football Hall of Fame. His play at Columbia University had earned him entrance into the College Football Hall of Fame.

Text of Letter from Sid Luckman to this Author, Dated June 30th, 1973

In a letter to me dated June 30, 1973, Sid Luckman revealed his position on Jewish issues as they affect professional sports. "No, I was not aware of any special following from Jewish fans or any other ethnic group," he wrote. "As for exercising influence as a spokesman about Jewish or any issues, I am not, nor ever was an orator, and always left this to political figures or heads of government," he added.

Luckman next explained why: "My talents were strictly athletic, and whenever called upon to speak publicly it was always in relation to my sport and the people connected with it. As athletes, I don't think we are qualified, or well enough informed to voice opinion on the grave issues you mentioned (the Holocaust and 1972 Munich murders of Israeli athletes by Arab terrorists)."

Using me as a point of reference, Sid Luckman elaborated: "You are a young man and must remember my playing years were before, during, and just after World War II. Before the 'Bill of Rights,' 'Women's Lib,' and the rest that might be making it more difficult *now* for a Jewish or black athlete, or one of Polish, Irish, or German extraction. But during my time, the fans were all for the game and applauded and appreciated a bright or clever maneuver and booed an error or stupid play.

"I do not think the Munich tragedy is a threat to American Jewish athletes any more than it is a threat to any Jewish athlete from any nation. I'm sure that in all future games involving nations, there will be tighter security to insure the safety of the participants; but, as I said before, I do not feel that the Munich affair poses any threat to Jewish athletes, American or otherwise."

But even the optimistic Sid Luckman expressed concern: "There have been fanatics and terrorists since the beginning of time, and although we all hope for the day when all people can live together in peace, I guess we'll always have fanatics and terrorists."

Luckman again reflected upon his era in concluding that in the forties "an individual was judged by his ability to perform, his sportsmanship—good or bad—and his talent in his particular field."

Because professional football during the Luckman era had not yet gained the same level of importance to society as baseball and because Luckman himself had not fully emerged as a superstar in that secondary sport when baseball slugger Hank Greenberg left the spotlight suddenly for nearly five years of military service, Luckman never

(Photo courtesy of the Chicago Bears)

attracted a visible Jewish following. Unlike Greenberg, Luckman fulfilled virtually all of his military obligations during his off seasons. Before the 1944 season, Luckman spent more than six months as a Merchant Marine on a tanker in the high seas. So while Greenberg was away, another very special Jewish athlete burst into stardom. Like Hank Greenberg, this athlete—Sid Luckman—had no idea that the quota system prohibiting entry into the United States of European Jews was resulting in their slaughter; or that concentration camps in Germany were butchering Jewish people by the millions. In contrast to how a visible segment of American Jewry collectively basked in the reflected glory of Hank Greenberg's home runs, the spectacular touchdown passes from the arm of Sid Luckman went comparatively unnoticed to an American Jewry that was suddenly distracted—distracted by the horrible truth suddenly emerging about Auschwitz, about Buchenwald, about Dachau, about Mauthausen, about Sachsenhausen, and about Treblinka.

To appreciate the magnitude of the impact Sid Luckman's successful introduction of the T formation had on modern football, with every team eventually adopting it, consider what might have happened if Luckman had signed with one of the major league baseball teams that had scouted him as shortstop during his brilliant tenure at Columbia University. If Luckman had experienced the same level of success in baseball that he did as a football quarterback for 12 seasons with the Chicago Bears, it is not too presumptuous to imagine that the nature of professional football and professional baseball would be vastly different and that the lives of countless sports team owners, managers, coaches, and players would have taken remarkably different turns.

Former Bears' owner George Halas designed the T formation for a quarterback with a strong and accurate throwing arm. This revolutionized a previously run-oriented game structured around a single wing formation. By successfully implementing the new strategy, Sid Luckman changed the complexion of football forever.

In the old single wing formation, the center snaps the ball to a left halfback or fullback—generally for a power sweep behind the blocking of a quarterback and right halfback. Frequently, the initial running back would lateral to one running just behind. In a single wing formation, such as this, which is unbalanced to the right, the right halfback lines up behind the right end and the blocking quarterback might line up behind the right guard such that either the fullback or left halfback are in position to receive a snap from the center—who is situated closer to the left end rather than at the middle of the line. A lineup such as that was designed primarily to facilitate a running attack.

The single wing offense dominated football until Sid Luckman introduced the T formation, in which the center hands the ball under his legs to the quarterback who might fake a handoff to a halfback or fullback and drop back to pass in search of a receiver. Some T formations have featured left and right halfbacks lined up in front of a fullback directly behind the quarterback, while others spread one and even two of the runningbacks as wide receivers.

Now, consider what might have happened if some other player had been given Luckman's opportunity and failed where Luckman succeeded; and if Sid Luckman had chosen baseball over football and experienced the same magnitude of success.

These imaginary time capsules show the way it might have been:

1939—Sid Luckman joins baseball's Cincinnati Reds midway through the season, but does not play until the fourth game of the World Series. With the New York Yankees winning three games to none, the Reds insert rookie Luckman into their starting lineup at shortstop in place of Billy Myers—who had been playing well, despite the Yankees' commanding advantage. Luckman—positioned in a new T formation behind second base—surprises critics by responding with errorless fielding and five hits over the last four games to help the Cincinnati Reds become the first team to win a World Series after losing the first three games. Later that year the Chicago Bears become the laughing stock of the National Football League by introducing a strange new quarterback system called the T formation. After five consecutive humiliating defeats, the Bears abandon the T formation and it is never heard of in football again.

1946—The Cincinnati Reds win their fifth pennant and fourth World Series in eight years; almost every team in baseball has adopted the T formation. The Chicago Bears finish last in their division for the eighth year in a row; owner George Halas sells the team to Howard Hughes, who promptly moves it to Las Vegas.

1965—Sid Luckman is elected into the Major League Baseball Hall of Fame.

But, maybe it's better the way it really was:

1939—Sid Luckman joined football's Chicago Bears and introduced the T formation. Baseball's New York Yankees swept the World Series in four games when Cincinnati Reds shortstop Billy Myers's ninth inning mess-up of a would-be double play and tenth inning error brought them from behind to win the final game.

1946—The Chicago Bears won their fifth divisional title and fourth World Championship in eight years on a surprise 19-yard run by quarterback Sid Luckman in the fourth quarter of the championship game; almost every team in football had adopted the T formation. Baseball's Cincinnati Reds were in the sixth year of a 21-year wait before their next World Series.

1965—Sid Luckman was elected into the National Football League Hall of Fame; he had earned the nickname Mr. Quarterback with an amazing passing record.

By changing the entire complexion of the sport that would someday surpass baseball as the national pastime with awesome championship performances and because of his introduction of the T formation—Sid Luckman has earned the distinction as the greatest quarterback ever to play football at a professional level and as the number two ranked Jewish athlete of all time.

Sid Luckman's Career Record

Year	Attempts	Completed	Intercepted	Yards	Touchdowns
1939	51	23	3	636	5
1940	105	48	9	941	6
1941	119	68	6	1181	9
1942	105	57	13	1023	10
1943	202	110	12	2194	28
1944	143	71	11	1018	11
1945	217	117	10	1725	14
1946	229	110	16	1826	17
1947	323	176	31	2712	24
1948	163	89	14	1047	13
1949	50	22	3	200	1
1950	37	13	2	180	1
Totals	**1744**	**904**	**130**	**14683**	**139**

In addition to his regular-season records, Luckman compiled an extraordinary record in championship games:

Year	Opponent	Score	Attempts	Completed	Yards	Touchdowns
1940	Washington	73-0 win	4	3	88	1
1941	New York	37-9 win	12	9	160	0
1942	Washington	14-6 loss	12	5	2	0
1943	Washington	41-21 win	26	15	276	5
1946	New York	24-14 win	22	9	144	1
Totals			76	41	670	7

"He was suave, debonair, extremely clever, and a good puncher, as well. He had patent leather hair always neatly combed; and the legend about him was that you were in your greatest trouble when you ruffled his hair. His boxing set a pattern . . ."—Barney Kremenko, sports writer, reflecting for me on how he remembered the World Lightweight Champion. (Photo courtesy of *The Ring Magazine*)

BENNY LEONARD

From all accouts, indications are that history's greatest pound-for-pound boxer might well have been one who fought under the last name of Leonard—not Sugar Ray, but Benny; and he was Jewish. The Ghetto Wizard, as Benny Leonard was known, won the World Lightweight Boxing Championship on May 28, 1917 and achieved a rare accomplishment for a boxer by retiring as champion on January 15, 1925 only to make a successful comeback as a welterweight from September 9, 1931 through October 7, 1932.

In *Nat Fleischer's Ring Record Book and Boxing Encyclopedia,* 1962, Fleischer had this to say about Benny Leonard: "He fought the greatest lightweights and welterweights of his period and was recognized as one of the greatest scientific fighters and most talkative boxer of modern times . . . He could jab and feint his way out of trouble, and if that wouldn't suffice, he would talk his way out of a jam. . . . He was a master on offense as well as defense." Fleischer was author of the book, *Leonard the Magnificent,* published shortly after Leonard entered the Boxing Hall of Fame in 1955.

During the summer of 1974, I launched a nationwide search for nominations to my proposed Jewish Sports Hall of Fame. In a letter to me dated August 9, 1974, Max Taub—Secretary-Treasurer of the B'nai B'rith Sports Lodge—wrote: "Your letter re 'Jewish Sports Hall of Fame' has been referred to me for reply." Among the members of the Sports Lodge to whom Max Taub referred me was the veteran of a nearly fifty-year sports writing career, Barney Kremenko, then Director of Public Relations for the American Basketball Association New York Nets. The first athlete Barney Kremenko nominated was Benny Leonard.

"I think Benny Leonard made the strongest impact of any Jew in boxing," Kremenko wrote. Then, he explained why: "Leonard, coming from the East Side of New York, was the World Lightweight Champion in the early twenties. He was suave, debonair, extremely clever, and a good puncher as well. He had patent leather hair always neatly combed; and the legend about him was that you were in your greatest trouble when you ruffled his hair. His boxing set a pattern and it is my belief that Sugar Ray Robinson later became the ultimate Benny Leonard."

It apparently was Benny Leonard that *Sporting News* reporter Frederick G. Lieb had in mind in his September 12, 1935 article on baseball slugger Hank Greenberg when he wrote: "It was my contention the Jew did not possess the background of sport which was the heritage of the Irish. For centuries, the Jew, in his individual business, had to fight against heavy odds for his success. It sharpened his wit and made him quick with his hands. Therefore, he became an individualist in sport, a skillful boxer and ring strategist, but he did not have the background to stand out in a sport which is so essentially a team game as baseball."

Of course, the relatively smaller representation of Jews preceding Hank Greenberg in team sports as compared to the number of Jews exemplified by Benny Leonard as engaging in individual athletic competition would have been better explained if Lieb had at least raised the possibility that systemic discrimination could have been a contributing cause.

What Lieb presented was nothing more than the type of plausible but unfounded generalization that would be directed at black athletes by Los Angeles Dodger executive Al Campanis in 1987 and CBS Sports commentator Jimmy "The Greek" Snyder in 1988 resulting in their dismissals after complaints lodged by civil rights extremist Jesse Jackson—a minister who ironically had on numerous occasions himself made unfounded generalizations alleging "Jewish" domination of the press, "Jewish" control of labor unions, and "Jewish" exploitation of black fighters. So to draw a comparison of the legendary Benny Leonard, who was credited by Nat Fleischer—then the world's foremost boxing authority—as being one of the most scientific fighters ever, with the larger and undoubtedly faster Sugar Ray Leonard, a great black champion of the modern era, runs the risk of implying an unintended racial generalization. The risk becomes readily apparent when the result of such a comparison concludes that, in a mythical match, Benny Leonard's uncanny ring savvy might have been enough to compensate for his physical disadvantage and enough to defeat Sugar Ray.

A mythical match between the two Leonards creates the illusion of an impending collision between irresistible force in Sugar Ray Leonard and the immovable force in Benny Leonard. To set the stage, first look for similarities in Benny Leonard's style and level of performance with that of Sugar Ray Leonard's four toughest opponents—Wilfredo Benitez in 1979, Robert Duran in 1980, Thomas Hearns in 1981, and Marvin Hagler in 1987. Remember that Benny Leonard, as depicted by Nat Fleischer, "was a master on offense as well as devense." An examination of Benny Leonard's career record shows that he scored 65 knockouts. According to Fleischer, Benny Leonard would "jab and feint his way out of trouble."

Of all Sugar Ray Leonard's opponents, Wilfredo Benitez presented the most scientific style. Like Benny Leonard, Benitz would jab and feint his way out of trouble. But unlike Benny Leonard, Benitez lacked sufficient punching power to keep the aggressive Sugar Ray at bay. After a tactical struggle, Sugar Ray Leonard opened up with a barrage of uncontested punches on Benitez that prompted the referee to stop the match just moments before it was scheduled to end in the fifteenth round.

For a projection of how Benny Leonard compared with the top opponents of Sugar Ray Leonard, a cross between the defensive skills of Wilfredo Benitez and offensive pursuit of Robert Duran emerges as an over-simplified conception of the Jewish legend. The result, in terms of how Benny Leonard would be expected to fare against Sugar Ray Leonard, is inconclusive. Sugar Ray Leonard experienced considerable difficulty against a Wilfredo Benitez who lacked the offensive pursuit of Roberto Duran; and Sugar Ray lost against a Roberto Duran who did not have the defensive skills of Wilfredo Benitez.

The closest analogy of an actual Benny Leonard opponent to the size and style of Sugar Ray Leonard was Welterweight Champion Jack Britton. Lightweight Champion Benny Leonard stepped up in weight for a title fight against Britton, who was close in size with Sugar Ray. Again the result was inconclusive. Benny Leonard struck with a sudden knockdown of Britton, but then was disqualified.

The question lingers whether Benny Leonard or Sugar Ray would prevail in a mythical match transcending time barriers to each fighter's prime. Put both Leonards in the same era and you'd have the largest sporting revenue in history and perhaps another landmark battle bearing a name like "The Thrilla in Manila" between Joe Frazier and Muhammad Ali or "The Brawl in Montreal" between this same Sugar Ray Leonard and Roberto Duran. Since no actual arena could house such a bout, it must be settled here. This is the way it might have been:

Electricity fills the air. It is "The Rumble in the District of Columbal." Both principles are in superb shape. Sugar Ray Leonard towers at least four inches over his Jewish opponent as the referee gives instructions. Pre-fight comments have created an aura of hostility. There is no love lost between the fighters—both of them great in their own right—here to take part in the ultimate dream match. Robert F. Kennedy Stadium glistens with celebrities. Benny Leonard pushes Sugar Ray, who must have said something. The referee tries to separate them. There's the bell. We're under way!

Round One. Five, six, seven straight jabs from Sugar Ray land flush on Benny Leonard's face already creating a red area above Benny Leonard's right eye. Sugar Ray thrusts his face as an open target for Benny Leonard. Sugar Ray winds his right arm but lands another left jab instead. He's clowning. It's all Sugar Ray. Benny Leonard tries to charge in but gets pushed back. Sugar Ray thrusts his face . . . AND BENNY LEONARD HITS IT with a sharp left jab. Oh! A tremendous right hand by Benny Leonard. Down goes Sugar Ray! Down goes Sugar Ray! Unbelievable. Sugar Ray Leonard is up at eight. But, he is hurt. That right hand hurt Sugar Ray. Now another right hand lead from Benny Leonard. Sugar Ray's knees wobble. He looks ready to go. Benny Leonard misses with a wild right cross. And Sugar Ray counters with a left hook. Down goes Benny Leonard. Benny Leonard is up at the count of four. But, Sugar Ray is all over him with a spectacular flurry—a barrage of punches coming from all directions. Benny Leonard is down again. He is down for the second time. The three-knockdown rule is in effect. Benny Leonard rises to his feet. Sugar Ray is trying to end it right here. A solid right from Sugar Ray shakes Benny Leonard. Sugar Ray lands another hard right. Benny Leonard ties up Sugar Ray AND LANDS AN UNBELIEVABLE RIGHT UPPERCUT. Oh! Sugar Ray is down flat on his back. And there is the bell ending round one. On all three judges' cards, the first round goes to Sugar Ray Leonard. It doesn't seem possible that either fighter can last the full 15 rounds.

Round Two. The pace slackens, but Benny Leonard is clearly the aggressor scoring several times with impressive body shots. Benny Leonard wins the round on all three judges' cards.

Rounds Three through Six. Sugar Ray is able to consistently evade the charging Benny Leonard, who bobs and weaves throwing wild left hooks. Few solid punches are landed and no damage is done to either fighter; but, Sugar Ray Leonard wins all four rounds.

Round Seven. Sugar Ray opens up a cut over Benny Leonard's right eye, who jabs and feints his way out of trouble without going down. The cut concerns Benny Leonard's corner men, who frantically try to stop it from bleeding. The round goes to Sugar Ray Leonard.

Rounds Eight through 10. Sugar Ray attempts to reopen the cut but is unable to land a direct hit. Benny Leonard masterfully dodges most of Sugar Ray's blows. But, both rounds go to Sugar Ray Leonard. Benny Leonard clearly needs a knockout to win.

Round 11. Sugar Ray finally reaches the patched area above Benny Leonard's right eye with a right-hand lead. Benny Leonard is bleeding profusely. The referee asks attending physicians to examine Benny Leonard's cut. Benny Leonard pleads for the referee and physicians not to stop the fight. The round ends. Round 11 goes to Sugar Ray Leonard. The crowd is on its feet collectively emitting a thunderous roar. Sugar Ray's corner people are looking for the signal that the fight is over. Fans in anticipation of the fight being called are cheering both fighters now. But, Benny Leonard is up to answer the bell with blood trickling down the side of his face.

Round 12. Sugar Ray moves in quickly for the kill with a flurry of punches. Benny Leonard misses with a wild left hook BUT LANDS A HARD RIGHT TO THE JAW OF SUGAR RAY. Oh! Sugar Ray counters with a stiff right. The punch is returned by Benny Leonard. The two warriors are trading punches too rapidly to call. A left hand by Sugar Ray staggers Benny Leonard. Sugar Ray misses with a right AND CATCHES A TREMENDOUS RIGHT HAND FROM BENNY LEONARD DROPPING HIM IMMEDIATELY TO THE CANVAS SLUMPED IN A NEUTRAL CORNER. Blood is pouring down Benny Leonard's face. He is unrecognizable. Sugar Ray struggles to his feet. No! He falls backward. The referee has counted Sugar Ray out. It's over! BENNY LEONARD HAS KNOCKED SUGAR RAY LEONARD OUT!

Sugar Ray, back on his feet, wraps both arms around Benny Leonard. The fighters embrace. It was a "Rumble in the District of Columbal."

That was the way it could have been.

The projection of Benny Leonard emerging victorious from a mythical match against Sugar Ray Leonard is an amazing tribute to the Jewish fighter who stood some four inches shorter and twenty pounds lighter. Benny Leonard was pound for pound the best. This five-foot, five-inch teenager, at 130 pounds, stepped into a boxing ring and helped refute the stereotype of "the weakling Jew."

In *Nat Fleischer's Ring Record Book and Boxing Encyclopedia,* only a turn-of-the-century fighter who died before Benny Leonard would fight his first professional bout, Joe Gans, finished higher among lightweights in Fleischer's All-Time Ranking of World Boxers. To appreciate the implications of that assessment, consider that the legendary Sugar Ray Robinson—at nearly six feet, the champion to whom sportswriter Barney Kremenko referred as the "ultimate Benny Leonard"—finished only fifth among middleweights, or one notch higher than Joe Louis rated among heavyweights. For his astounding longevity as World Lightweight Champion and trend-setting style, this pioneer among Jewish athletes is ranked as the third greatest Jewish athlete of all time.

SANDY KOUFAX

Because his last name has evolved into an adjective most frequently used when attempting to succinctly describe the highest possible level of performance by a baseball pitcher, many people tend to forget or do not realize that when Sandy Koufax announced his retirement—on November 18, 1966—he was only thirty years old. Early in his career, Koufax would hurl the ball at a frightening velocity without reliable control. When he mastered control of a lightning quick fast ball and sudden curve, he was virtually unhittable. Koufax created a unique aura of fear and anticipation—the fear of sudden death by the sickening thought of a batter being struck by a ball traveling at that speed and anticipation of witnessing a perfect game or no hitter. Koufax attributed the incredibly premature retirement to an arthritic condition in his left elbow that had forced him to miss a considerable amount of playing time, often put him in agony on the pitching mound, and jeopardized his future well-being to the extent that he already had to shorten the left sleeve of his sports jackets. But, in addition, his nearly total domination of batters had to make the game less and less challenging.

When Koufax entered the National Baseball Hall of Fame at Cooperstown, in 1972, he joined Hank Greenberg as the second Jewish player inducted. His plaque tells why: "SET ALL-TIME RECORDS WITH 4 NO-HITTERS IN 4 YEARS, CAPPED BY 1965 PERFECT GAME, AND BY CAPTURING EARNED-RUN TITLE FIVE SEASONS IN A ROW, 1962–1966. WON 25 OR MORE GAMES THREE TIMES. HAD 11 SHUTOUTS IN 1963. STRIKE OUT LEADER FOUR TIMES, WITH RECORD 382 IN 1965. FANNED 18 IN A GAME TWICE. MOST VALUABLE PLAYER 1963. CY YOUNG AWARD WINNER 1963–65–66."

I reached Sandy Koufax in East Holden, Maine, in 1973, and posed questions to him regarding the impact of the Munich murders of Israeli athletes on American Jewish athletes, disparate treatment he may have experienced because of his being Jewish, and the appropriateness of Jewish athletes using their fame to promote the public's support of Jewish causes. In a letter to me postmarked May 12, 1973, Koufax responded: "I hope you will understand when I say . . . my personal feelings have always remained private and I would prefer to keep it that way." That desire for privacy was consistent with a Koufax mystique described by 1966 biographer Jerry Mitchell: "A shy guy, the public has thought Koufax aloof . . . . To his Los Angeles teammates, he is . . . a bit of a loner who moves about mostly by himself." But, Mitchell emphasized that Koufax's teammates considered him "a class guy" and "good company" when he was around them.

In 1966—the same year as Jerry Mitchell's biography—Koufax published an autobiography with Ed Linn. That autobiography offered a rare glimpse of Koufax's Jewish heritage. "The Jewish Community House on Bay Parkway . . . became my second home," Koufax wrote with reference to his high school years. Ironically, Koufax received an athletic scholarship at the University of Cincinnati for basketball and averaged nearly 10 points per game in his only year there as a rebounder. Unlike Mitchell's book, the autobiography explained why Koufax upset the Dodger's pitching rotation by sitting out the first game of the 1965 World Series: "Yom Kippur is the holiest day of the Jewish religion. The club knows that I don't work that day."

The publicity surrounding Koufax's decision not to open the World Series in 1965 because it fell on Yom Kippur helped demonstrate the sanctity of that day for a public opinion that would react with shocked horror at the unified attack of Israel eight years later without provocation by Arab forces. Perhaps if Koufax had pitched that day, President Richard M. Nixon might not have understood the despicability of the Arab attack and might not have been as quick to put American forces on alert. And today, ordinary working Jewish people might experience more difficulty when attempting to take time away from their jobs in observance of the Day of Atonement.

On November 6, 1975—almost ten years to the date Sandy Koufax demonstrated the sanctity of Yom Kippur—*The Washington Star* ran a banner sports headline reporting: "Parkdale Coach Suspended for Practicing on Religious Holiday." The story went ont to report that Tom Rae, one of the metropolitan Washington area's most successful high school football coaches, was suspended from coaching for one week without pay for holding a team practice on the Jewish New Year, Rosh Hashanah even though none of the players on his team was of the Jewish faith. The story quoted Rae as saying: "I made a mistake." The article made no mention of Sandy Koufax or of any other famous Jewish athletes. But a decision by Koufax ten years earlier to have pitched on Yom Kippur—which is even a holier day than Rosh Hashanah—could have set a precedent that would have easily justified Rae's decision. While gentile recognition of Rosh Hashanah or Yom Kippur has not evolved into a tradition to the extent that it generally exerts an impact upon schedule-making, the sanctity of the day for Jewish people is not in question.

In 1960, Sandy Koufax had not yet arrived as baseball's greatest pitcher. But that year—on among the greatest of Jewish days, one even perhaps as heroic as the subsequent rescue of Israeli hostages in the now legendary raid on Entebbe—Koufax celebrated with his first one-hitter. The date was May 23, 1960. Hours before the game, Israeli Prime Minister Ben-Gurion, in a voice full of emotion, read the following statement: "Adolf Eichmann is already under arrest in Israel and he will shortly be

Less than a month before Arab terrorists would murder eleven Israeli athletes at the 1972 Olympiad in Germany, Sandy Koufax became the second Jewish player to make the Baseball Hall of Fame. Here, Koufax flashes a World Series ring and a miniature version of his Hall of Fame plaque. The baseball commissioner looks on. (Photo courtesy of the Los Angeles Dodgers)

brought to trial in Israel under the Nazis and Nazi Collaborators Law of 1950." In the second inning of a game between the Pittsburgh Pirates and Los Angeles Dodgers that night, Pirate batter Benny Daniels slapped a clean single. The pitcher was Sandy Koufax. That would be the only hit Koufax would give up that night.

Until now no comparison had ever been made between the simultaneous announcement of Eichmann's capture and the extraordinary accomplishment by this Jewish pitcher. Whether the breakthrough *coup de grace* by Nazi hunter Simon Wisenthal in outsmarting the German bureaucrat responsible for contributing to the murder of six million Jewish people inspired Sandy Koufax is purely a matter of conjecture. But, on that night—after learning with the rest of the world of Adolf Eichmann's capture—Sandy Koufax was not to be denied. This was a turning point in Jewish history. Eichmann was eventually executed; and Sandy Koufax became immortal.

Linking the emergence of Sandy Koufax to the highly publicized heroic capture of Adolf Eichmann by Simon Wiesenthal might conflict with the pitcher's own humble assessment. But, at the time of Eichmann's capture, Koufax had an inauspicious record of 28 games won and 31 games lost. The night Eichmann was apprehended, Koufax pitched a spectacular one-hit shutout. From that point on—including the one hitter—Sandy Koufax compiled an astronomical 119–43 won/lost record. Just about then, his self-confidence began to blossom. Whether the greatness of Simon Wiesenthal inspired Sandy Koufax to recognize his own enormous talent—whether that special sense of pride. and' extended feeling of personal accomplishment swelling so many Jewish people had an effect on Sandy Koufax—is something perhaps that even Koufax could not answer.

Sandy Koufax blended unprecedented physical talent, extreme intelligence, self-confidence, and a trait that enabled him to fulfill his vast potential. That trait was uncompromised dedication. In his book, *Koufax* with Ed Linn, Sandy Koufax exhibited that uncompromised dedication in this passage: "I have never believed in fraternizing with the players on other teams, because the guys in the other uniforms are your enemies and I see no reason to get to know an enemy well enough to have any feeling other than sheer hostility toward him."

Perhaps it was just another coincidence. But shortly after Sandy Koufax retired, major league baseball found itself irrevocably being overtaken by professional football as the most popular sport in the country. Was the inevitably downward trend in baseball excitement caused by Koufax's departure just the opportunity professional football needed to exploit its electrifying merger between established and unconventionally new leagues? When Koufax announced his retirement, the Associated Press quoted then Dodger manager Walter Alston as saying: "He was probably the greatest pitcher ever in baseball." That sounds like an extreme understatement compared to some of the quotes cited in Jerry Mitchell's unauthorized biography published at the height of Koufax's career.

New York mets manager Casey Stengel was quoted by Mitchell as saying: "Umpires often can't see where Koufax's pitches go so they have to judge from the sound of them hitting the catcher's glove." Mitchell quoted former baseball executive Paul Richards as contending that Koufax could "beat a team made up of the nine best players in the history of baseball."

Like Hank Greenberg, Sid Luckman, and Benny Leonard—Jewish athletes who set standards for brilliance in their sports—Sandy Koufax has carved a new dimension of success that has earned him the elite distinction of fourth place in this Jewish Sports Hall of Fame's All-Time Athletic Rankings

Koufax created a unique aura of fear and anticipation—the fear of sudden death by the sickening thought of a batter being struck by a ball traveling at a frightening velocity and anticipation of witnessing a perfect game or no hitter. (Photo courtesy of the Los Angeles Dodgers)

When Sandy Koufax retired, he took so much American folklore with him that for the first time the sport could no longer sustain its status as the nation's favorite pastime and professional football took over—perhaps forever. Sandy Koufax exuded a magic making him forever symbolic of his times.

Sandy Koufax's Career Pitching Record

Team Year	Innings	Strikeouts	Wins	Losses	Earned Run Average
Brooklyn 1955 - 57 and Los Angeles 1958 - 66 Dodgers	2324	2396	165	87	2.76

SANDY KOUFAX'S FIVE BEST YEARS

1962	184	216	14	7	2.54
1963	311	306	25	5	1.88
1964	223	223	19	5	1.74
1965	336	382	26	8	2.04
1966	322	317	27	9	1.73
COMPOSITE	275	289	22	7	1.95

Box Scores of Sandy Koufax's Four No Hitters

LOS ANGELES, JUNE 30, 1962 - -

NEW YORK METS	at bats	hits
Asburn lf	3	0
Kanehl 3b	4	0
Mantilla 2b	3	0
Thomas 1b	2	0
Cook rf	3	0
Hickman cf	3	0
Chacon ss	2	0
Cannizzaro c	3	0
R. Miller p	0	0
Daviault p	2	0
Woodling ph	0	0
Christopher ph	0	0
Totals	25	0

New York Mets..000 000 000 - 0
Los Angeles Dodgers.....................................400 000 10x - 5

LOS ANGELES, MAY 11, 1963 --

SAN FRANCISCO GIANTS	at bats	hits
Kuenn lf	4	0
F. Alou rf	3	0
Mays cf	3	0
Cepeda 1b	3	0
Bailey c	2	0
Davenport 3b	3	0
Amalfitano 2b	3	0
Pagan ss	3	0
Marichal p	2	0
Pregenzer p	0	0
McCovey ph	0	0
Totals	26	0

San Francisco Giants 000 000 000--0
Los Angeles Dodgers 010 003 04x--8

PHILADELPHIA, JUNE 4, 1964 - -

PHILADELPHIA PHILLIES	at bats	hits
Rojas cf	3	0
Callison rf	3	0
Allen 3b	2	0
Cater lf	3	0
Triandos c	3	0
Sievers 1b	3	0
Taylor 2b	3	0
Amaro ss	3	0
Short p	2	0
Roebuck p	0	0
Culp p	0	0
Wine ph	1	0
Totals	**26**	**0**

Los Angeles Dodgers	000 000 300 - - 3	
Philadelphia Phillies	000 000 000 - - 0	

LOS ANGELES, SEPTEMBER 10, 1965 - -
   (The Perfect Game)

CHICAGO CUBS	at bats	hits
Young cf	3	0
Beckert 2b	3	0
Williams rf	3	0
Santo 3b	3	0
Banks 1b	3	0
Browne lf	3	0
Krug c	3	0
Kessinger ss	2	0
Amalfitano ph	1	0
Hendley p	2	0
Kuenn ph	1	0
Totals	**27**	**0**

Chicago Cubs	000 000 000 -- 0	
Los Angeles Dodgers	000 001 00x -- 1	

DOLPH SCHAYES

His standing among the greatest players in the history of basketball was nearly as illustrious as that of baseball's Hank Greenberg, who challanged the left-handed swinging Babe Ruth and clearly emerged as the greatest of all right-handed hitters; Sid Luckman, who changed the way that professional football was played and launched a passing attack comparable to the best modern day quarterbacks while also playing defense; Benny Leonard, who dominated the lightweight boxing division to such an extent that he eventually had to retire in his prime because of a lack of competition; and Sandy Koufax, who totally intimidated hitters by pitching a baseball so fast that it gave the illusion of crossing a sonic barrier—each of whom has a legitimate claim to having been the best ever to perform at his position, or in the case of Leonard his weight class. Dolph Schayes was the best power forward in basketball history.

When proposing a mythical all-time professional basketball team, it inevitably comes down to tough decisions such as Oscar Robertson over Magic Johnson or Bob Cousy as the ball handling guard, Jerry West over Pete Maravich or Michael Jordan at shooting guard, Wilt Chamberlain over Akeem Olajuwon or Bill Russell at center, Larry Bird over John Havlicek or Julius Erving at quick side forward, and Kevin McHale or Elvin Hayes at power forward behind Dolph Schayes.

Mere statistical differences between the records compiled by basketball players from different periods fail to demonstrate a valid and reliable comparison of their abilities. Informal tolerance of traveling violations, added prohibitions against a zone defense, stricter interpretation of personal fouls, introduction of the three-point shot, and other significant rule changes have dramatically increased the amount of scoring in games since the fifties—the Dolph Schayes era. Virtually every flying drive of the type made famous by Julius Erving and later Michael Jordan actually exceeds the prescribed limits on movement by a player while holding the ball but it is now tolerated to add excitement to the game. Without the zone defense, ball handlers such as Magic Johnson can more readily find an open man inadvertently released from difficult to sustain man-to-man coverage. Post players such as Kevin McHale pile up on extra point shots for fouls that would likely not have been called during the Schayes era. Long distance bombers such as Larry Bird pad their statistics with the extra point not awarded for a long two-handed set shot by Dolph Schayes. A more meaningful way to compare basketball players of different periods is to consider how they ranked in various categories with their contemporaries. When it came to scoring and rebounding—the ingredients of a pure power forward—Dolph Schayes ranked among the best year after year.

By the time the National Basketball Hall of Fame inducted Schayes for his performance on the court in 1972, he had already completed a successful second career as a head coach. As a player, Dolph Schayes could do it all—shoot long distance with amazing accuracy from either hand, drive for power layup baskets, rebound off either the defensive or offensive boards, pinpoint precision passes, and play defense one on one. When he retired, no player had been elected to more first or second All National

Basketball Association teams—having placed on the first team in the 1951–52, 1952–53, 1954–55, 1956–57, and 1957–58 campaigns; and on the second team in the 1949–50, 1950–51, 1955–56, 1958–59, 1959–60, and 1960–61 campaigns. In the 1948–49 season, Schayes was voted Rookie of the Year. The following season, he ranked sixth in scoring and sixth in assists.

He took the name Adolph out of the gutter and made it an adjective for precision in basketball during the fifties. The ambidextrous forward established himself as the most explosive offensive threat professional basketball would see until seven-foot centers emerged the following decade. But, the offensive grace of Dolph Schayes merely complemented his extraordinary rebounding and all-around defensive greatness. The spectacular Schayes played nearly ten years without missing a single game. After his fabulous playing career, the Dolph Schayes legend continued with a brilliant coaching career. The National Basketball Hall of Fame would induct the six-foot, eight-inch superstar and—along with earlier basketball great, Nat Holman—Jews could claim two of the greatest who ever played the game. (Photo courtesy of the Buffalo Braves)

It was not until the 1950–51 season that the league compiled records for individual rebounds. Schayes led the league in rebounding that year and finished seventh in scoring. For the next decade, Schayes would compete for league leadership in scoring, rebounds, assists, and free throws. With the rebounding of an Elvin Hayes, inside scoring of Kevin McHale, long distance shooting of Larry Bird, and passing accuracy of a Magic Johnson—Dolph Schayes will forever represent a prototype for the consummate power forward in professional basketball. His son, Danny, grew into a nearly seven-foot center in the National Basketball Association. At some three inches taller than his celebrated father, the younger Schayes never developed his father's graceful scoring and shooting touch. But, like his father, Danny Schayes developed into a feared rebounder and key man on the fast break with a tenacious outlet pass that earned him a place in this Jewish Sports Hall of Fame and a ranking in the top third of the Fifth Jewish Supreme Fourteen on his own accord.

When I first set out to establish a Jewish Sports Hall of Fame, I reached Dolph Schayes in De Witt, New York. In a letter to me postmarked December 27, 1973, Dolph Schayes reflected upon his perception of the impact of Jewish people participating in professional sports. "There aren't enough Jews in sports," he wrote. "But, Jewish athletes do perform a valuable public relations service for American Jews," he added.

According to Schayes: "Obviously, American Jews take pride in accomplishments of successful Jewish athletes, not only on a national level but down the line in high school." He expressed definitive thoughts about the question regarding whether prominent athletes can exert a meaningful impact on public opinion by speaking out on political issues. "Public opinion is influenced by attention-getters—whether they be athletes, clergymen, or politicians—speaking intelligently on any issue," he responded.

Dolph Schayes dismissed the issue of prejudice by flatly indicating: "Prejudice, for the most part, has left the American sports scene at all levels." Keep in mind that he made the statement almost fifteen years before the relatively low proportion of black baseball managers and football head coaches would surface as a sensitive issue culminating in the controversial dismissals of Los Angeles Dodger executive Al Campanis and football television analyst Jimmy "The Greek" Snyder for making public comments that, in effect, justified the domination of white people in those positions. Dolph Schayes was responding to a question directed primarily at Jewish athletes who have a smaller representation than blacks in going on to coach or manage professional teams after their playing days are over. Then, Schayes added: "In fact, most teams are on the lookout for Jewish athletes."

Finally, Dolph Schayes turned his attention to the unforgettable nightmare of Munich in 1972 when eleven Israeli athletes were murdered by Arab terrorists. He saw no direct implication from that incident to American Jews who compete in sports. "There is no terrorism threat to a Jewish athlete competing in the United States," he concluded.

A patented Dolph Schayes drive to the basket had the awesome power of a Hank Greenberg home run. His ability to play offense and defense equally as well evoked memories of the versatile football quarterback Sid Luckman, who would stay on the field to play defense or on special teams. His incredible durability was reminiscent of Benny Leonard's reign as World Lightweight Boxing Champion. And from long distance, his two-handed jump shot had the glitter of a Sandy Koufax strikeout. Each of these five Jewish athletes—Greenberg, Luckman, Leonard, Koufax, and Schayes—defined the standard for excellence at a critical position or competitive weight class in his sport. These are the five greatest Jewish athletes in history.

RON MIX

While most people familiar with the old American Football League credit flamboyant quarterback Joe Namath with forcing its eventual merger with the National Football League, some former players attribute the junior league's stability to the man many consider to be the greatest offensive lineman in professional football history—the Intellectual Assassin, Ron Mix, for his conduct on and off the field. Mix would go on to join professional football's greatest quarterback, Sid Luckman, as the second Jewish member of the Pro Football Hall of Fame. By then, Mix had built a second career as an attorney and sports executive.

The offensive line, where Mix played for more than a decade, is known in football circles as the trenches where a game is won or lost. No other position of any sport requires the incumbent to react as quickly, hit as hard, and bear as much repetitive punishment. By gaining constant recognition as arguably the most fierce-hitting immovable force to ever play the game and publicly associating himself with his heritage, Ron Mix demolished any reminders from the Jewish stereotype created by the Holocaust of a debilitated weakling defending himself with only an arsenal of cliches.

After earning All-America honors as team captain for the University of Southern California, he emerged as the number-one draft choice of both the established National Football League's Baltimore Colts and the fledgling American Football League's Los Angeles Chargers. Following in the footsteps of the poet Robert Frost, Ron Mix "took the road less traveled by, and that has made all the difference." The Los Angeles Chargers quickly became the San Diego Chargers and the American Football League eventually became part of the National Football League. In the distant future, long after Mix retired, the Baltimore Colts would become the Indianapolis Colts. But, one thing never changed—for ten years with the Chargers and long after as a lasting memory, Ron Mix was a symbol of strength. He retired to complete law school, only to make a surprise return and be traded by the Chargers to the Oakland Raiders for whom he played two more years. Nine times he was selected to the All-League Team. He played in seven All-Star and five Championship Games.

In a letter to me dated June 26, 1973, Ron Mix reflected upon his special following from Jewish fans, implications of the Munich tragedy on other Jewish athletes, and prejudice. First, he addressed his Jewish following: "Allow me to preface my answer with the observation that the general mass of people admire daring, courage, and tenacity. This admiration is even directed to those who pull off an unusual criminal act."

Then, Mix turned to the Jewish stereotype of not being athletically inclined. "Intellectual accomplishment has never been among the most honored qualities," he wrote. "Indeed, the general feeling is that physical prowess and intellectual accomplishment are mutually exclusive," he added. Mix related the distinction in perception between physical prowess and intellectual accomplishment directly to the Jewish stereotype: "It has been part of the Jewish stereotype to equate Jews with intellectuals; ergo, not then equated with physical prowess."

Ron Mix's nickname, the Intellectual Assassin, reflects the public's recognition of him as a tough guy on the field and smart one off it. "Well, Jews take the same pride in physical accomplishment as others and thus have been undoubtedly troubled by this phase of their stereotype, just as they have been troubled by other phases," noted Mix.

The name Ron Mix symbolizes a real-life Dirty Harry—a Jewish Dirty Harry, who would be even more convincing than actor Clint Eastwood in saying: "Go ahead, make my day" to Josef Mengele, to Yasser Arafat, and to Louis Farrakhan. (Photo courtesy of the San Diego Chargers)

He added: "Thus, the Jew is likely to take a racial pride in the accomplishments of a Jewish athlete. I have witnessed this during my career as a professional football player. Jewish youngsters and adults have approached me and were clearly pleased that I was a Jewish athlete."

Mix then extended his point by drawing an analogy between Jewish athletes and the fighting men and women of Israel: "To carry this observation further, but cast it in a different light, witness the great pride world Jewry takes in the accomplishments of Israel and in the collective Israeli reputation for hard work, fighting, courage, and daring. The emergence of Israel has completely changed the stereotype of the Jew and allowed him to function comfortably in American society."

Mix raised questions regarding the value of younger people basking in reflected glory: "In the end, however, I would caution young people that there is no personal merit in the accomplishments of others. For a minority group, racial pride is inevitable. But realistically, the achievements of others do not make the non-achieving observer any better. One must look to themselves and take pride in their own work, their own attitudes, and actions."

I had asked Mix if he felt Jewish superstars had a responsibility to use their influence as spokesmen for other American Jews about critical issues such as the Holocaust or the Munich murders. Ron Mix recalled a quotation of which he could not name its author or guarantee the precise wording: " 'There is no guarantee that tomorrow you will not be a victim of an injustice you allow to exist today.' " According to Mix, "All people have a responsibility to call attention to injustices that exist anywhere within world society. That one is a potential victim, of course, makes the interest in doing so more personal; but, the fervor should be the same." Then, he acknowledged: "We truly do live within a world community wherein isolated events affect all eventually. Thus, there is a selfish reason to correct injustices even if one is motivated altruistically."

Finally, he revealed his opinion: "Public figures have a podium not reserved for others and their efforts—even if not in degree any greater than that of others—have a wider span of influence. Yes, Jewish superstars should use this podium to the same extent as their peers of other faiths."

I also asked Mix if he considered the Munich tragedy a threat to other Jewish athletes. "The threat is a possibility but by no means omnipresent. The Arab terrorist groups are apparently sensitive to public opinion and because the world reaction was unanimously condemning, the terrorist groups undoubtedly saw themselves losing any hopes of building world sympthay for their cause," he wrote. Then, he attempted to analyze the problem: "I feel the terrorist groups, and the people they claim to represent—the Palestinian Arabs—are being misled by many of the Arab leaders in order to draw attention away from the real problems that face the unfortunate mass of Arabs."

Ron Mix saw the problem as a matter of economics: "The real problem appears to be that great wealth is centered in the hands of realtively few in much of the Arab world. The wealth of the Arab world is such that were there adequate distribution, much of the mass poverty could be alleviated."

But, he noted that solving the problem is easier said than done. "Like all privileged classes in any country, the wealthy few wish to protect their holdings. As long as the Israelis command the attentions of the masses, the masses do not give attention to their internal problems," he wrote. He added: "The great poverty within many of the Arab nations concerns me and I would like to see an effort made to dramatically better the living conditions of the average Arab."

Finally, I asked Ron Mix if he encountered any prejudice. "When one is young, most encounters of prejudice are imagined because one is sensitive to being different; and I experienced the same discomfort when one imagines himself to be in a foreign situation—in my case, a Jew within a predominantly Christian country," he responded. But, then he added: "This feeling lasts only until the one belonging to the minority group matures enough to realize that if some people harbor general prejudices against others then that is their problem."

And how did the Intellectual Assassin advise other famous Jewish athletes to deal with prejudice should they encounter it? "Each of us is important simply because we exist and our worth is measured by moral standards and ethical behavior," he began, with some advice intended for non-athletes as well. "Identification with a group does not change one's intrinsic character. If one feels that others believe this, then that person should not feetl uncomfortable, nor feel somehow that he is inadequate. Rather, he should simply acknowledge that there exists some screwed-up thinking in this world," he concluded.

Because football offensive linemen only have their names called for penalties and they don't compile individual statistics from which fans could track their progress through newspapers, the name Ron Mix never became embedded in American culture to the extent that the names of less successful athletes who had the benefit of playing more glamorous positions have. But, Ron Mix symbolizes a real-life Dirty Harry—a Jewish Dirty Harry, who would be even more convincing than actor Clint Eastwood in saying: "Go ahead, make my day" to Josef Mengele, to Yasser Arafat, and to Louis Farrakhan. The publicized fact that this Jewish athlete made the Pro Football Hall of Fame on the basis of pure brute force at an unskilled position in an upstart league far away from major media centers, reinforced an extreme contradiction of a weakling ethnic stereotype in the minds of many who followed professional football in the sixties; and the impact of that will forever linger. For that reason he ranks as the sixth greatest Jewish athlete ever—ahead of many names made more famous by virtue of their more glamourous positions—Ron Mix proved once and for all that tough guys can finish first.

After serving as executive counsel of the San Diego Chargers, Mix jumped once again to an upstart league—the World Football League—as general manager of the Portland Storm entry. This time the new league failed. But, Mix's decision to again assume the risk of an uncharted course demonstrates the unrelenting ambition that made Ron Mix an imovable force.

(Photo courtesy of the Oakland A's, by Ron Riesterer)

During Ken Holtzman's first three Oakland years—each of which resulted in a World Series Championship for the A's—he averaged 20 regular season victories plus victories in both the League Championship Series and the World Series. By the time he was thirty, he had six seasons in which he had won 17 or more games, two no-hitters, and 165 regular season games won. He belongs in the National Baseball Hall of Fame; but, he may never make it.

KEN HOLTZMAN

The year was 1976. At thirty, Ken Holtzman had already won 165 regular season games, two League Championship games, and four World Series games; compiled stunning earned run averages of 2.06 in League Championship games and 2.55 in World Series games; and pitched two no-hitters and numerous near misses. His arm was sound and he was about to enter his prime in New York—as a Jewish pitching star, having recently been acquired by the Yankees—in the League Championship series. But for some inexplicable reason, Yankee manager Billy Martin held Ken Holtzman out of that series—which the Yankees won. Then, it was off to the World Series with Ken Holtzman as the anticipated starting pitcher. It would be Holtzman's fourth World Series in which he would be the opening game pitcher. It was not to be. Not only did Billy Martin keep Holtzman out of the first game, he kept Holtzman on the bench for the entire World Series watching as the Yankees went down to defeat. Unbelievable.

Coming into the season in which Holtzman was dealt to Martin's Yankees, the Jewish lefthander had averaged more than 19 regular season wins per year over four years with the Oakland A's. In his split season with the Baltimore Orioles and Yankees, Holtzman won 14 games. Six times he had won 17 or more games with the Athletics and Chicago Cubs, for whom he compiled a perfect nine win season while on release from National Guard duty his second season in the Major Leagues. He was on his way to a 300 win career and the National Baseball Hall of Fame; or, so it seemed. In fact, when I originally set out to establish a Jewish Sports Hall of Fame, I raised that very question with a man who had managed against both Holtzman and Sandy Koufax. In a letter to me postmarked June 25, 1973, former San Francisco Giant manager Herman Franks, who was not Jewish—when posed the question regarding whether he expected Holtzman to join Koufax in the National Baseball Hall of Fame after his playing days were over—responded: "Yes, I think both pitchers should be in the Hall of Fame." This is the same Ken Holtzman about whom Oakland A's owner Charley O. Finley proclaimed on national television in 1973: "Without you (Holtzman), we couldn't have won two World Series in a row. G-d bless you. With you, we're going to make it three World Series wins in a row." Finley was right. Holtzman did pitch the A's to their third consecutive World Championship the following year. Then, free agency destroyed what could have rivaled the New York Yankees as baseball's greatest dynasty when several players fled the team.

After excluding Holtzman from the 1976 League Championship and World Series games, Billy Martin continued not to use his strong armed southpaw in the 1977 season—a season in which the Jewish pitcher managed to slip into enough games to compile a shocking record of two wins and three losses. Needless to say, Billy Martin again kept the healthy Holtzman out of that season's League Championship and World Series games. As incredible as it may seem, the following season was even worse for Ken Holtzman. In 1978, Billy Martin continued his inexplicable practice of keeping the great pitcher out of action. After winning his only decision for the Yankees, the rusty and demoralized Ken Holtzman was dealt to the Chicago Cubs. Holtzman was not the same pitcher. He retired after the following season.

(Photo courtesy of the Oakland A's)

In February of 1988, I talked in-depth with a former member of that Yankee team about Holtzman's forced inactivity. Elliott Maddox, a black center fielder who told me that he had converted to Judaism in 1974 but was not a Zionist, confirmed that Holtzman was strong armed and healthy during the entire period in which Billy Martin refused to use him. Maddox stated that he believed the prolonged inactivity destroyed Holtzman's career, but volunteered that he saw no indication of anti-Semitic discrimination or prejudice of any kind by Martin. Martin did play the team's other two Jewish players—Maddox and Ron Blomberg—and there is no evidence that has been made public implicating Martin of discriminatory behavior then or any other time.

Because I talked with Maddox during the 1988 presidential campaign at the height of conflicting values between Jews and blacks, I attempted to capture an insight of his unique perception as a highly visible representative of both groups. Maddox refused to either agree or disagree with follow-up statements I sent him, which in effect speculated whether he would have perceived discrimination in the situation had Holtzman been black; if being a non-Zionist meant that he would not be disturbed if Yasser Arafat were to take political control of Israel provided that the Jews there were granted religious freedom; and whether he experienced inner conflict as a black Jew in the face of what many Jewish people considered offensive acts by black leaders—such as Jesse Jackson's highly publicized charges that there is "Jewish domination of the press," "Jewish control of labor unions," and "Jewish boxing promoters exploiting black fighters" and his use at the slur "Hymie" when referring collectively to the Jewish People—which prompted Nathan Perlmutter, National Director of the Anti-Defamation League of B'nai B'rith, to describe Jackson as "a person whose recorded expressions are those of an anti-Semite." Despite all this, Maddox was unequivocal in his stated devotion to his Jewish religion and in his apparent respect for the pitching ability of Ken Holtzman.

The day after the Jewish New Year in 1966, then rookie Kenneth Dale Holtzman was slated to pitch against the legendary Sandy Koufax. Holtzman rocked the baseball world with a nearly perfect game, handing the more famous Jewish southpaw what would be his last regular season defeat. Of course, Holtzman went on to pitch two no-hitters, many near no-hitters, three consecutive shutouts, a string of 33 consecutive scoreless innings, two League Championship victories, four World Series victories, and a workhorse number of innings; he batted .333 in World Series play, including a home run; and he built an indisputable reputation for winning in the clutch—all until he had the misfortune of playing for a manager with whom he had an apparent personality conflict. He was on his way to compiling 300 career wins. But, it was not to be.

In a letter to me postmarked April 28, 1973, Ken Holtzman addressed the subject of prejudice some two-and-a-half years before his ill-fated trade to the Yankees so without any implied reference to Billy Martin. "Nobody feels the sting of prejudice like some professional athletes," he wrote. Then he added: "One day—when I'm out of the game—I'll tell it like it was."

Then Holtzman focused on the impact of the murder in Munich of 11 members of the Israeli Olympic team the year before. "The night I learned about Munich was the night before I was to pitch in Chicago. I was with Mike Epstein and—needless to say—we were shocked," he recalled. "I think we felt angry at first and then grief," he added. At the time of the Munich murders, Ken Holtzman was leading his Oakland Athletics through a highly publicized pennant race that would culminate in their first of three consecutive World Series Championships.

Holtzman, though far removed and not in the mortal danger that confronted Olympic hero Mark Spitz—a Jewish swimmer, who had just won an unprecedented seven gold medals—faced a similar decision to that which confronted Spitz. In the previous olympiad, which took place during a period of black activism in the United States, medalist John Carlos held his fist in a so-called "black Power" salute to demonstrate his support of the unrest to his fellow black Americans.

Many journalists led the public to anticipate some sort of symbolic gesture from Spitz that never materialized. In the summer of 1987, I had an indepth conversation with Spitz's father-in-law, Herman Weiner, who advised me that Spitz was never in a position to publicly demonstrate his outrage and grief because of security restrictions placed upon him as the tragedy unfolded.

This is Ken Holtzman's recollection of his decision: "We knew some crackpot could be after one of us. We decided to wear black armbands the next day at the game, although neither of us felt like playing. We wore the bands for about a week, realizing this could mark us. But, it didn't matter."

Holtzman's gesture was appreciated. Soon after the Munich murders, Israel decided to resume sending its athletic teams abroad. When the Israel National Basketball Team competed in the World Student Games in Moscow, Soviet officials led mobs to harass the Israeli team and physically attack Russians who rooted for them. In February 1974, the Israeli team visited Washington, D.C. for a game against Catholic University—which Israeli easily defeated in a mismatch. Israeli coach Avraham Hemmo specifically recalled Ken Holtzman pitching with an armband in demonstration against the Arab terrorists. Hemmo told me: "We were aware Holtzman and the other Jewish-American athletes felt for their brothers who died in Munich. We go anywhere in the world to play; we prove we're not afraid. We want to live like anyone has a right to live. We won't stay home afraid. All of us are fighters on the front line."

Box Scores of Ken Holtzman's Two No-Hitters

Chicago, August 19, 1969 --

ATLANTA BRAVES	at bats	hits
Alou cf	4	0
Millan 2b	4	0
H. Aaron rf	4	0
Carty lf	2	0
Cepeda 1b	3	0
Boyer 3b	3	0
Didier c	2	0
Garrido ss	2	0
Niekro p	2	0
T. Aaron ph	1	0
Niebauer p	0	0
Totals	27	0

Atlanta Braves .... 000 000 000 - 0

Chicago Cubs .... 300 000 00x - 3

CINCINNATI, JUNE 3, 1971 --

CINCINNATI REDS	at bats	hits
McRae lf	3	0
Helms 2b	4	0
L. May 1b	3	0
Bench c	3	0
T. Perez 3b	3	0
Foster cf	3	0
Bradford rf	1	0
Concepcion ss	3	0
Nolan p	2	0
Ferrara ph	1	0
Gibbon p	0	0
Totals	**26**	**0**

Chicago Cubs .... 001 000 000 - 1

Cincinnati Reds .... 000 000 000 - 0

KEN HOLTZMAN'S CAREER PITCHING RECORD

Team Year	Innings	Strikeouts	Wins	Losses	E.R.A.
Chicago Cubs 1965 - 71, 78 - 79	2,867	1,601	174	150	3.49
Oakland 1972 - 75					
Baltimore 1976					
New York Yankees 1976 - 78					

KEN HOLTZMAN'S FIVE BEST YEARS

1970	288	202	17	11	3.38
1972	265	134	19	11	2.51
1973	297	157	21	13	2.97
1974	255	117	19	17	3.07
1975	266	122	18	14	3.14
Composite	**274**	**146**	**19**	**13**	**3.02**

Ken Holtzman adds the missing piece to the Jewish Magnificent Seven—Greenberg, Luckman, Leonard, Koufax, Schayes, Mix, and Holtzman—the seven best Jewish athletes of all time. To appreciate the actual value of Ken Holtzman in comparison with other major contributors from two of baseball's greatest teams—the 1961 New York Yankees featuring Mickey Mantle, Roger Maris, and Yogi Berra and the 1972 Oakland A's featuring Jim "Catfish" Hunter, Holtzman, and Reggie Jackson—you can track the calculation of his ranking among these players from the Pay For Performance Baseball Compensation System that I created. This study was published in the September 1981 issue of the *Journal of Systems Management*.

The Economics of Baseball

Acquiring a professional sports franchise requires a monetary outlay of the magnitude reserved for the business elite—and the amounts paid are usually determined by intuitive speculation. Not surprisingly, these owners use a whimsical pay-for-potential compensation system for their athletes. De-emphasizing actual performance and paid attendance is not the best method of motivating their athletes to compete and entertain. Consequently, team owners realize reduced returns on their investments in atheletes.

Pay for Potential (The Economics of Baseball)

Major League Baseball compensation is surprisingly unfair, with differences as large as 400 percent common between salaries of seemingly equivalent performers. Despite controlling a monopoly on their players' services, baseball team owners perpetuate an unhealthy cycle. Players insist on preposterous long-term contracts as the price for not submitting their demands into binding arbitration. After a productive year, many players insist on even more exorbitant renegotiated contracts as the price for not sitting out the following year. After playing for a certain amount of time, players can sell their services to other teams as free agents. To avoid losing these players at the expiration of their contracts, most baseball executives propose staggering contract extensions. As a result, salaries range from less than $100,000 to more than $2,500,000 per year—sometimes without any apparent justification. Just 30 years ago, Roger Maris held out for a salary of less than $50,000 per year after winning the 1960 Major League's Most Valuable Player Award. Inflation expands today's value of that 1961 salary to $300,000 per year. But because of today's wild salaries this is considered unsubstantial in Major League Baseball. Today, Ken Holtzman would receive a salary ranging anywhere between $900,000 and $1,800,000 per year. Finally, another problem is that teams are now bidding wildly for free agents.

Pay for Performance (The Economics of Baseball)

Without a salary structure, free agents create an imbalance of talent among teams and disproportionate salaries among players. Ironically, each baseball game generates enough meaningful statistics indicative of both individual and team performance to establish a model compensation system adaptable for the entire sports industry.[1] This author introduced such a system. The system would benefit owners by facilitating salary control, a balance of talent, and increased player responsiveness to the paying public. Players would benefit from more equitable salaries, total freedom of movement among teams without incurring obligation on either new or previous owners, and elimination of the need for high commissioned agents. In addition, the public would benefit from lower ticket prices. The system would not interfere with owners' television and radio revenue or players' endorsement and media income. *Ken Holtzman could have escaped from Billy Martin.*

The model compensation system establishes a base salary for all players similar to the varying grades of the federal government's General Schedule, which undergoes comparability adjustments each October to keep pace with the private sector. Using this system there would be a $41,121 base salary for the 1989 baseball season. The system arrives at salaries by linking performance statistics from the previous year to a matrix, which determines the relative portion of a pay pool for each player after multiplication by a position adjustment factor. A team's pay pool size would depend upon the average paid attendance and lowest ticket price throughout the league and its own winning percentage, such that:

Rationing pay pools among teams induces a balance of talent through natural migration of top performers to teams with less internal competition for salary increases. With attendance serving as the primary basis for determining pay pool sizes, players would gain incentive to entertain their patron fans. The system rewards owners for reducing ticket prices, by linking team payrolls to their lowest priced tickets. The league could establish a standard two-dollar ticket price at all stadiums for unreserved seats. Adjusting the attendance-base pay pools by each team's winning percentage would increase the level of competition on the field.

Matrices would establish relative values for combinations of statistics compiled by the league during the previous year. Each pitcher earns a point value based upon his number of games won and earned-run average. Every other player receives a point value based upon his number of home runs and batting average.

The position adjustment factor takes into account the number of games started, games off the bench, fielding average, and relative position difficulty. The pitcher ranks as the most difficult position, followed by catcher, shortstop, second baseman, center fielder, right fielder, third baseman, left fielder, first baseman, and designated or pinch hitter. *As a pitcher, Ken Holtzman would have been directly compensated for number of starts, wins, earned run average, and fielding average.*

Testing the System

Simulations demonstrate the feasibility of this model system. The 1962 New York Yankees and 1973 Oakland A's offer the most extreme example of contrasting team compositions. The 1961 World Champion Yankees featured a select group of extraordinary performers surrounded by an average supporting cast. Depending more on consistency rather than on the heroics of a few top performers, the 1972 World Champion A's emerged as the epitome of team play. This simulation compensates the 1962 Yankees and 1973 A's for their previous years' accomplishments.

In 1961, the New York Yankees compiled a .673 regular season winning percentage. In 1972, the Oakland A's finished the regular season with a .600 winning percentage. For the purpose of this simulation, assume both teams compiled their respective records in the 1980 season; that both teams reduced prices of their lowest cost seats to two dollars per ticket; and that paid attendance throughout the league averaged 1,000,000 fans. For the 1981 season, each New York Yankee player would receive a base salary of $32,048 (step 1 of grade 13 under the October 1980–September 1981 federal General Schedule) plus a performance-based portion of a $3,346,000 pay pool ($2 \times 1,000,000 \times 1.673 = 3,346,000$). Each player on the Oakland A's would receive a base salary of $32,048 and a performance-based portion of a $3,200,000 pay pool ($2 \times 1,000,000 \times 1.600 = 3,200,000$). To impute the amounts at an approximate 1989 value; simply MULTIPLY EACH FIGURE BY ONE-AND-A-HALF with the exception of the step 1 of a grade 13 federal government salary, which only advanced about half as much to a $41,121 rate. That represents a typical journeyman level for a nonsupervisory position in the federal government.

Applying the Matrices

Within the performance matrix for pitchers, each cell infers a relative point value for specified combinations of games won and earned-run averages. The point value rises with an increase in the number of games won, but declines with an increase in earned-run average. Figure I displays the performance matrix for pitchers. The matrix requires no computations to arrive at a point value. *For example, Ken Holtzman's 19 win and 2.51 earned-run average performance in 1972 would convert to a matrix value of 7 points.*

Within the performance matrix for non-pitchers, each cell infers a point value for specified combinations of homeruns and batting averages. The point value rises with an increase in either home runs or batting average. For example, Mickey Mantle's 54 homerun and .317 batting average performance in 1961 converts to a matrix value of 8 points. Figure II exhibits the matrix for non-pitchers.

Adjusting Matrix Values

A position adjustment factor transforms the matrix point value into the player's relative number of pay pool shares. Each player receives itemized credit for games started or entered in progress, weighted by a relative position difficulty index. Figure III illustrates. Players receive no point adjustments for position changes during the progress of a game. Multiplying the total weighted credits by the player's fielding average—if applicable—produces the position adjustment factor. For example, Elston Howard compiled a .993 fielding average in 1961 as starting catcher in 111 games and a .989 fielding average as starting first baseman in 9 games. He came off the bench in 9 games as a pinch hitter. These data yield a position adjustment factor of 180.17:

$(111 \times 1.5 \times .993) + 9 \times 1.111 \times .989) + (9 \times .55) = 180.17$

Howard's 21 home run and .348 batting average performance for the Yankees in 1961 converts to a matrix value of 6 points. Multiplying Howard's 6 point performance matrix value by his 180.17 position adjustment factor yields a total of 1081.02 pay points. Figures IV and V document simulated pay point distributions for all of the New York Yankees and Oakland A's, respectively. *Only Mickey Mantle, Jim "Catfish" Hunter, Roger Maris, and Elston Howard compiled more pay points than Ken Holtzman.*

Converting Pay Points into Dollars

Dividing a team's cumulative pay points into its pay pool establishes the monetary value of a pay point. For example, the simulation produced a $3,346,000 pay pool for the New York Yankees. As shown in Figure IV, the Yankees compiled a total of 8,946.12 pay points in the simulation. Dividing $3,346,000 by 8,946.12 yields a $374.02 value for each pay point. In the simulation, Yankee Cletis Boyer earned 165.18 pay points for 11 home runs, a .224 batting average, .967 fielding average in 141 games as starting third baseman, and 1.000 fielding average in 7 games as starting shortstop. Multiplying the $374.02 point value by Boyer's 165.18 point total produces a performance payout of $61,780.62. Adding the $32,048 base salary to Boyer's $61,780.62 performance payout results in a $93,828.62 total salary in 1981 dollars.

The simulation produced a $3,200,000 pay pool for the Oakland A's. Table V shows a simulated compilation of 7,118.70 pay points by the A's. Dividing $3,200,000 by 7,118.7 yields a $449.52 value for each pay point. The simulation converted 15 home runs, a .236 batting average, .960 fielding average in 151 games as starting third baseman, and .500 fielding average off the bench in one game at second base by Oakland's Sal Bando into 166.25 pay points. Multiplying the $449.52 point value by Bando's 166.25 point total produces a performance payout of $74,732.70. Adding the $32,048 base salary yields a $106,780.70 total salary. Figures VI and VII display simulated salary breakdowns for the entire Yankees and A's rosters, respectively. *Ken Holtzman would have earned a higher salary than such legendary players as Whitey Ford, Reggie Jackson. Rollie Fingers, and Yogi Berra.*

Bonus earnings

The system provides players with an opportunity to earn supplemental income in addition to customary shares of playoff and World Series receipts. Each of the two leagues would establish million-dollar funds annually. In each league, the fund would attach lucrative bonuses to each of the previously nonmonetary honors perennially associated with baseball tradition.

Most Valuable Player Awards would earn both league recipients bonuses of $100,000; Cy Young (top pitcher) Award recipients would earn bonuses of $100,000; and Rookie of the Year Award recipients $50,000. Sports writers would select these recipients. The nine (including pitcher) fan-elected All-Star Game starters would receive $25,000. Official statistics would determine the remaining recipients. Qualified fielding average leaders (nine) would receive $25,000; highest winning pitchers $50,000; qualified earned-run average leaders (lowest average) $50,000; fireman title winners (relief pitchers with the highest totals of saves and wins) $50,000; home run leaders $50,000; qualified batting average leaders (highest average) $50,000; and runs batted in leaders $50,000—all of which represent 1981 dollars. In 1989, these bonuses would be one-and-a-half times as large.

Movement Restrictions

Players would have from the day after the World Series in October until December 31 to sign with the team of their choice, if different from their current team. Team owners would have until January 31 to either automatically renew the contracts of holdover players or release them for tryouts with other teams in spring training. The system would prohibit any trades or sales of players without prior written consent by the players involved. Teams would have only until the end of spring training to conduct player transactions. No longer could long-term contracts bind the services of top performers to a particular team. Insensitive or unresponsive team owners could offer no fringe benefits to lure better players. A more permissive style of management would emerge. *No Billy Martin could ever again destroy the career of a Kenny Holtzman.*

Evaluation

With this proposed system in effect, many top performers would move to weaker clubs for higher salaries. The simulated payrolls show Yankee third baseman Cletis Boyer making almost $13,000 less than comparably performing Oakland third baseman Sal Bando. Both Yankees Roger Maris and Elston Howard compile approximately the same number of pay points as Oakland's Jim Hunter; but, Hunter makes nearly $85,000 more than Maris and more than $87,000 more than Howard. The presence of several top performers on the Yankee roster reduces the relative salaries of supporting players. Oakland's more evenly distributed performance payout would have provided the top performing Yankees with significantly higher salaries had they played for the A's, despite the larger pay pool of the Yankees.

On weaker teams, a single top performer could earn the bulk of his team's entire pay pool. But, only for one season. The weaker team would attract more top performers, creating a natural balance of talent throughout the league. In all probability, the simulated Yankee team would have lost at least one if not two of their three highest salaried performers to weaker teams at the season's end. But, once a natural balance of talent was achieved, massive player movements would stop. The sport would regain the spotlight from its finances. Once again, players and the paying public would concentrate on baseball.

This simulation of the baseball version of my sports compensation system, known in professional literature as The Silverman System, not only provides pay equity for athletes but a quantified ranking of their actual value to their teams. Here, two of baseball's legendary championship teams were simulated: the awesome 1961 New York Yankees and 1973 Oakland A's, on which Ken Holtzman compiled 19 wins—the composite average for his five best years; not his best year, but an average good one. For that, he compiled 790.51 pay points.

The list of Hall of Famers and future Hall of Famers compiling fewer pay points in Figures IV and V, for the Yankees and A's respectively, is staggering. On the Yankees, ace southpaw Whitey Ford finished with 752.64 after his greatest year; Yogi Berra compiled 509.80 pay points. On the A's, slugger Reggie Jackson had 611.92 pay points and the great relief pitcher Rollie Fingers 585.00 pay points. The players who compiled more pay points than Ken Holtzman form an exclusive list—Mickey Mantle, Jim "Catfish" Hunter, Roger Maris, and Elston Howard.

During Ken Holtzman's first three Oakland years—each of which resulted in a World Series Championship for the A's—he averaged 20 regular season victories plus victories in both the League Championship Series and the World Series. By the time he was thirty, he had six seasons in which he had won 17 or more games, two no-hitters, and 165 regular season games won. He belongs in the National Baseball Hall of Fame; but, he may never make it.

THE JEWISH-AMERICAN ALL-TIME ATHLETIC RANKINGS

The Jewish Second Superlative Seven

8. Benny Friedman
9. Johnny Kling
10. Al Rosen
11. Mark Spitz
12. Nat Holman
13. Abe Attell
14. Henry Wittenberg

(Photo courtesy of Benny Friedman)

BENNY FRIEDMAN

Considering that Sid Luckman retired as the greatest quarterback in football history, in the view of many authorities quoted in materials provided me by Pro Footfall Hall of Fame Librarian Jim Campbell, a frank assessment presented by Minnesota Viking President Max Winter in 1974 raises profound questions regarding why Benny Friedman was left out of the Pro Football Hall of Fame. Postmarked September 27, 1974, the letter to me from Max Winter first noted that Mark Spitz "had a great opportunity to assert himself on many issues, which would have been published around the world," with reference to the great swimmer's relatively low profile after winning seven gold medals at Munich when 11 Israeli athletes were murdered by Arab terrorists in 1972; and that—contradictory to my earlier assessment of Ron Mix—Winter "would not say that he was one of the greatest linemen ever to play the game." Max Winter conveyed frank and definitive opinions in that letter. That is why what he said about Benny Friedman takes on enormous significance: "As for a comparison of Sid Luckman, Benny Friedman, and Harry Newman (an All-America and Collegiate Player of the Year, rated number 32 in my Jewish-American All-Time Athletic Rankings because a devastating injury terminated his professional career halfway through his second year), it is unfair for me to rank them even though it was fortunate to see them all on several occasions. All three of them were very great quarterbacks and perhaps given the same chance to play on the same teams, I doubt that there could be a great comparison."

Benny Friedman was the first quarterback to launch a successful passing attack from the old single wing formation used before Sid Luckman's implementation of the T formation and had perhaps the most explosive passing offense at the college or professional levels until then. The legendary Notre Dame coach Knute Rockne, who would later be the subject of a movie starring Ronald Reagan (as dying football star George Gipp) that made famous the line "Win one for the Gipper," was quoted as recognizing a growing consensus of Benny Friedman as being the greatest passer of all time and offering his assessment of Friedman as being a standout runner and blocker as well. Friedman also gained recognition as an outstanding field goal kicker. From a college All-America to being the highest salaried professional player of his era, when he singlehandedly turned the New York Giants from a league doormat to a nearly undefeated powerhouse: Benny Friedman accumulated virtually every collegiate and professional honor with one exception—induction into the Pro Football Hall of Fame.

In a letter to me postmarked June 12, 1973—during the period in which I initially set out to establish a Jewish Sports Hall of Fame—Benny Friedman revealed no trace of bitterness over his inexplicable exclusion from the Pro Football Hall of Fame in Canton, Ohio. He indicated that he had never encountered any anti-Jewish experiences and generally stated that: "One gives and takes and performs and is recognized by his performance, not by any outside circumstances." At that time, the Pro Football Hall of Fame had only been in existence less than a decade. At that time, it would be conceivable to speculate that Benny Friedman still expected to gain entry. His personal letterhead displayed an illustration of a quarterback just over his name. But, somewhere along the line, he must have lost hope. He made several critical statements about his inexplicable exclusion and—just two days before Thanksgiving in 1982—he shot himself dead. Perhaps someday, the Pro Football Hall of Fame will find Benny

Friedman his rightful space. Ronald Reagan's final words as George Gipp would then take on special meaning for Benny Friedman: "I don't know where I'll be then, but I'll know about it and I'll be happy."

Text of Letter From Benny Friedman To This Author, Dated June 12, 1973

"There definitely was a Jewish following. Jews naturally look to those who are outstanding in a sport and identify with them. I believe that religion should be left private. A youngster or adult plays a game as a competitor, with no reflection about his faith. It just happens that one is a Jew or Catholic, or what not. I never felt that I was a spokesman. I did represent to the Jewish people a breakthrough when I was elected captain of Michigan, in 1926. The Jews were concerned about whether I would be elected, but I was not.

"I never was threatened and I never had any anti-Jewish experiences. My teammates and opponents were wonderful. In athletics, there is a common denominator of dedication to a team that transcends all else. One gives and takes and performs and is recognized by his performance, not by any outside circumstances.

"My mother helped me in her way by her faith. She would put 18¢ in the Pushke before I would leave for the ball game. She felt that 18—representing Chai, which means life—was needed in this charity gesture to protect me. I was never injured and I never questioned her about this representation of her faith. It worked."

JOHNNY KLING

The Jew in American sports forcibly divorces American Jewry from the unfortunate image of powerless weaklings. Because the public exhibits a distinct pattern of judging a whole people's caliber on the physical prowess of their most gifted individuals—a trait acquired in grade school—Jewish athletes transfer their acclaim to American Jewry, who obligingly bask in reflected glory. So a deliberate decision by a successful Jewish athlete to publicize or conceal his or her religion exerts a direct impact upon the collective image of American Jewry. Occasionally, there comes a gifted individual who the public mistakenly identifies as Jewish. When the individual allows that impression to continue, that individual becomes as valuable a contributor to the cause of contradicting an unflattering Jewish stereotype as those who are actually Jewish. Such an individual was Johnny Kling.

The misconception that this turn-of-the-century catcher was Jewish has evolved so strongly that modern writers on Jews in sports have unwittingly perpetuated the myth despite their stated intentions of adhering to strict definitions of Judaism in their coverage of athletes. There is evidence that Kling led many to think he was Jewish.

Johnny Kling was not Jewish. In the September 12, 1935 issue of *Sporting News,* Frederick G. Lieb wrote: "Johnny Kling, capable Cub catcher of the days of Chance's great machine, was of part Jewish blood and for many years was placed at the top of the list by Hebrew fans. Were Johnny of full Hebrew blood, I would rank him next to Greenberg among the foremost Jewish players of all-time." To determine the origin of that part so-called Hebrew blood, I turned to the number one authority on baseball history. In a letter to me dated June 13, 1973, Ken Smith, Director of the National Baseball Hall of Fame, advised me that research by his librarian Jack Redding had revealed that Kling's "wife was of that faith."

While Johnny Kling's religion was a mystery to some, his catching ability was not. This is what Frederick G. Lieb wrote about him in the 1935 *Sporting News* article: "Not only was he a great mechanical catcher, a fine thrower, and good hitter, but he was one of the smartest of all ball players. Many considered him the brains of the great Cub machine."

Johnny Kling's base path battles with legendary stolen base champion Ty Cobb provided the high points of a game that seldom witnessed the home run. During the Johnny Kling era—from 1900 through 1913—home run leaders averaged about 10 a year very possibly because of a less lively ball. So, because of the similarity of names, a comparison between Kling and the modern day Johnny Bench that immediately comes to mind might in fact draw a realistic picture of the turn-of-the-century catcher. While the comparatively dead ball precludes a meaningful comparison of their power, Johnny Kling twice stole 23 bases in a single season—a feat Johnny Bench could never approach. Amazingly, Johnny Kling never grained entrance into the National Baseball Hall of Fame. Both catchers' plaques belong in Cooperstown.

Because tangible evidence suggests that Johnny Kling knowingly encouraged perpetuation of the myth that he was Jewish, he has earned the right to have his accomplishments rated against those of athletes who actually were Jewish—especially since he elected to do this in an era before civil rights of Jewish citizens were recognized. Conversely, the wire service story on pitching great Jim Palmer of October 6, 1966—when Palmer was slated to pitch against Sandy Koufax in the World Series in what would turn out to be Koufax's last game—that Palmer was born of, but not raised by, Jewish parents did not result in his inclusion in the Jewish Sports Hall of Fame. I included Johnny Kling because—from all indications—that is the way he would have wanted it.

(Photo courtesy of Al Rosen)

AL ROSEN

After the 1953 season, writers on Major League Baseball—for the second time—reached a unanimous selection for the American League Most Valuable Player. Al Rosen had made history after slugging 43 home runs, driving in 145 runs, and batting .336 as a standout third baseman. During the five seasons between 1950 and 1954, Rosen averaged better than 31 homers with 114 runs batted in while hitting at a better than .298 clip. These extraordinary statistics are particularly impressive for a third baseman. Yet, Al Rosen never made the National Baseball Hall of Fame through traditional voting. Perhaps an old timers' committee will muster enough votes for his induction—an induction his record clearly warrants.

Ironically, one hall of fame that did induct Al Rosen did so on the basis of his accomplishments as a football player. In a letter to me dated June 18, 1973, University of Miami Sports Publicity Director Bob Catchpole wrote: "His career here was limited to 1943 during the war . . . However, the Board of Directors saw fit to elect him to the University of Miami Sports Hall of Fame in early 1972."

Rosen's one spectacular season of college football as a two-way end earned him the nickname Flip. According to material provided to me from University of Miami archives by Bob Catchpole, "Flip was around long enough to be a big star on a team, which won five games and lost only to a powerful Jacksonville Navy team."

As for the identity of the first unanimous selection in either league for the Most Valuable Player award in Major League Baseball, it was Hank Greenberg.

In a letter to me dated July 5, 1973, Al Rosen expressed his opinion that "Jewish athletes, particularly because of the publicity given to their acts, should always be aware of their heritage and act accordingly."

Text of Letter From Al Rosen To This Author, Dated July 5, 1973

"There is no doubt that a Jewish athlete, if he has any degree of success in his career, picks up a large Jewish following. It is a warm feeling to demonstrate those ideas that can be exemplary amongst Jews.

"I have always attempted to be honest and forthright when questioned about the Jewish issues in the world. I have worked long and hard in the community at attempting to justify my existence and I feel that it is incumbent upon Jews everywhere to become well-known spokesmen for the Jewish religion. I feel that Jewish athletes, particularly because of the publicity given to their acts, should always be aware of their heritage and act accordingly."

MARK SPITZ

No athlete ever dominated an olympiad the way Mark Spitz did in 1972. He won seven gold medals in swimming—the 100-meter free style and butterfly, 200-meter freestyle and butterfly, a role in the 400-meter freestyle relay, a role in the 800-meter freestyle relay, and a role in the 400-meter medley relay-with record setting performances. The 22-year-old Indiana University graduate had exceeded by two the record number of gold medals previously compiled by an individual in a single olympiad. Perhaps it was the unwarranted expectation of others that created unnecessary complications for Mark Spitz.

The 1972 Olympics marked the first olympiad that would be held in Germany since the 1936 Olympics when black American medalist Jesse Owens humiliated Adolf Hitler with a record-setting performance. The highly publicized fact that Spitz was Jewish, when related to the irony that the olympiad in which he had starred had taken place in Germany, created expectations in many for some sort of symbolic gesture by Spitz to dramatize his accomplishments as a memorial to the six million Jews who fell victim to the Holocaust.

In the previous olympiad, black American medalist John Carlos had raised a defiant fist in a militant black power gesture to demonstrate what he perceived to be inequities experienced by blacks in the United States. That was in 1968, when tensions between blacks and whites reached a dangerous level of intensity.

Mark Spitz had become a household name. Suddenly, Arab terrorists murdered eleven Israelis at the Munich Olympics. Many of the journalists who had refrained from leading their readers or viewers to anticipate a definitive reaction from Mark Spitz for his having emerged as a hero in the very place where so many of his fellow Jews were slaughtered—in Germany—joined the growing band of reporters pressing Mark Spitz for statements as if he were a political rather than an athletic figure. The *1973 World Book Year Book,* the annual supplement to the *World Book Encyclopedia,* reported that "Spitz seemed curt and uninterested at news conferences, and he refused to pose with his seven medals for photographs (he sold the rights to a German magazine)."

In early June of 1987, I talked in depth with Herman Weiner, father-in-law of Mark Spitz, who explained that Mark was under such tight security that he was uanble to fully express his outrage and grief; and that Mark had continued to participate with the Jewish Olympic Maccabiah Games.

A 1984 fund raising letter from the United States Committee/Sports for Israel conveyed this message over the signature of Mark Spitz: "The excitement of meeting Jewish athletes from around the world, and sharing with them the universal spirit of sports competition, was a matchless experience. . . . I understand even better now what it means to Israel and to world Jewry."

Both in 1973—when I initially set out to establish a Jewish Sports Hall of Fame— and again in 1988, I was unable to obtain responses to my questions from Mark Spitz after numerous attempts. So, I discussed Spitz with other Jewish athletes who at one time found themselves under public scrutiny for their athletic accomplishments. There was no consensus regarding whether the attainment of fame carries with it a responsibility to use the resultant visibility in making known the interests of the group of which the athlete is a member, even if the athlete had been recipient of loyal support from that group. The various opinions appear verbatim within the context of the entire

(Photo courtesy of the William Morris Agency)

commentary of athletes who did respond to my questions. Perhaps the tendency of an individual to be outspoken or to withhold expressing his opinions dictates whether he or she should use the otherwise unavailable visibility that fame brings to speak out rather than any type of moral obligation passed on to someone because he or she is a member of a certain group that collectively holds the same opinions. Unfortunately, the relatively small number of Jewish athletes in the public eye at a given time casts a disproportionate amount of importance to each individual's decision.

There may have been a disproportionate amount of emphasis placed upon Spitz's still remarkable accomplishments. In a letter to me dated December 19, 1973, from Marilyn Ramenofsky—herself a 1964 Olympic silver medalist in swimming and my selection for seventeenth rank in the Jewish-American All-Time Athletic Rankings—wrote: "Medals are not awarded equally among all the sports; for example, there are many more medals given in swimming than in gymnastics." Nevertheless, Mark Spitz exploded in the public eye as demonstrably the greatest swimmer ever with one of the most spectacular athletic victories imaginable before a worldwide audience.

NAT HOLMAN

Considered possibly the greatest guard in professional basketball history, Nat Holman excelled in practically every high school sport—receiving honors in baseball, football and soccer in addition to basketball. But Holman would save his greatest accomplishments until his final years, when he emerged as president of the United States Committee on Sports for Israel. As a player: Holman was considered the most spectacular ballhandler ever to grace a basketball court; his team—the Original Celtics—drew acclaim as the greatest basketball dynasty until Red Auerbach molded the Boston Celtics nearly half a century later. But, his accomplishments for sports in Israel provided physical education and fitness for Israeli youth more comprehensive than they had experienced before. Every four years, the Committee sponsored the United States Maccabiah Team for participation in the World Maccabiah Games in Israel—a sponsorship that would never end. American-Jewish athletes could exchange their culture with Jews everywhere.

(Photo courtesy of Nat Holman)

Text of Letter From Nat Holman To This Author, Dated July 24, 1974

"During my career as a professional basketball player—especially when I was the only Jewish player on the Celtics—I was very much aware of the Jewish following that supported me in a number of cities on the circuit. While I always played at my very best, I tried even harder when I knew the Jewish community was rooting for me.

"I believe strongly that the outstanding performance of Jewish athletes has a profound effect on Jewish youth and adults as well as on non-Jews. Excellence in sports helps Jews to be even prouder of their great heritage so that they can keep their heads high without feeling inferior to any other group. It helps non-Jews to understand that Jews are not only 'people of the book' but that they also share in the wholesome interests and activities of all their fellows.

"I believe that Jewish athletes can be a powerful influence by setting examples and raising standards for youth and adults to achieve positive goals. Qualities developed in athletic competition are the same qualities essential for success in all walks of life. It is a major responsibility of all prominent Jewish athletes to dedicate themselves to partnership with the best interests and highest ideals of Jewish life.

"I do not fear the threat of terrorism against American Jewish athletes."

ABE ATTELL

In his 1962 *Ring Record Book and Boxing Encyclopedia,* legendary boxing authority Nat Fleischer rated Abe Attell as the third greatest featherweight boxer of all time behind second-ranked Jem Driscoll and number one ranked Terry McGovern. This ranking came despite the fact that, according to Fleischer, "his 10-round no decision with Jem Driscoll on February 19, 1909 at New York is rated as one of the best exhibitions of ring science ever seen in New York," and even though Attell never fought McGovern. This particular ranking of Fleischer's is especially puzzling because Driscoll never held the featherweight title and McGovern suffered a second-round knockout less than two years after he had won it. Attell, on the other hand, won the title with a knockout in 1904 and held it through 11 successful defenses until losing it on a 20-round decision in 1912. Abe Attell won his first 32 professional fights—24 by knockout. He may indeed have been the greatest World Featherweight Champion of all time. In 1955, he was inducted into the Boxing Hall of Fame.

Photo by Ring Magazine

Promoter Tex Rickard considered Abe Atel the "Little Champ" to be the greatest pound for pound fighter of all time.

Abe Attell

HENRY WITTENBERG

A light heavyweight freestyle Olympic wrestler, Henry Wittenberg emerged as a hero of two olympiads—the 1948 Olympics as a gold medalist and the 1952 Olympics as a silver medalist. In keeping with his Jewish heritage, he would later surface as wrestling coach of Yeshiva University. Ironically, Wittenberg's most publicized wrestling victory came not when he won the gold medal in 1948—but, when he captured the silver in the following olympiad. In winning the silver medal in 1952, Henry Wittenberg scored a dramatic upset victory over the reigning Russian world champion August Englas.

One can only imagine the impact of Wittenberg's combative success had it occurred in 1936 at Berlin in the presence of Adolf Hitler, or in 1972 at Munich with the joint stench of PLO assassins and the German military cemetery at Bitburg. Regardless of who Henry Wittenberg would have drawn as an opponent in Berlin or Munich—in that match—he would not have been denied. And if Wittenberg had defeated a world champion Russian in 1984 or 1988—periods in which Russian oppression of Jewish people had evolved into a major political issue—Jewish people everywhere would forever bask in reflected glory.

Henry Wittenberg came along some thirty years too early to cash in on his dramatic gold and silver medals. But, his roughhouse wrestling style did much to obliterate the weakling Jewish stereotype. (Photo courtesy of Yeshiva University by Herbert S. Sonnenfeld)

MITCH GAYLORD

Mitch Gaylord emerged in the 1984 Olympiad at Los Angeles as a multiple medal winner in the mold of 1972 swimming sensation Mark Spitz, but as a gymnast and without as much fanfare - - because there was no victimization of Jewish people unfolding as he performed and he did not perform where the Holocaust had taken place. Consequently, the fact that Mitch Gaylord was Jewish did not apparently come to the attention of the media.

Mitch Gaylord is the greatest Jewish gymnast ever. In 1984, he dazzled a worldwide live television audience with spectacular precision on the parallel bars, extraordinary grace on the horse vault, and brute force on the rings. Attempts to reach Mitch Gaylord through the United States Gymnastics Federation and his former agent were unsuccessful. But, his greatness has earned him a ranking in the Jewish Superlative Seven, tied with Henry Wittenberg for fourteenth rank.

During the 1984 Olympics, Mitch Gaylord won the Gold medal for Team Gymnastics, a Silver medal in Vaulting, and two Bronze medals, one for the Rings and one for theParallel Bars. That is particularly noteworthy when evaluated in context with the statement of 1964 Olympic swimming medalist Marilyn Ramenofsky that "many more medals are given in swimming than gymnastics."

MITCH GAYLORD, ONE OF THE
GREAT GYMNASTS OF ALL TIME

THE JEWISH-AMERICAN ALL-TIME ATHLETIC RANKINGS

The Jewish Second Supreme Fourteen

15. Max Zaslofsky
16. Ted Kid Lewis
17. Marilyn Ramenofsky
18. Dick Savitt
19. Nancy Lieberman
20. Steve Stone
21. Harold Solomon
22. Battling Levinsky
23. Andy Cohen
24. Sid Gordon
25. Brian Gottfried
26. Barney Ross
27. Julie Heldman
28. Brad Gilbert

MAX ZASLOFSKY

After retiring as the third highest scorer in the history of professional basketball, Max Zaslofsky seemed destined for induction into the National Basketball Hall of Fame. But as the years passed, it became evident that it was not to be. The inequity became obvious on the National Basketball Association's twenty-fifth anniversary. In a letter to me postmarked September 3, 1974, Zaslofsky proudly recalled that, he was selected along with 24 other players as the 25 best players in the NBA over the last 25 years.

In 1946, the Jewish forward placed third in the league in scoring and made All-League First Team. In the year that began in 1947, Max Zaslofsky again made All-League First Team as he led the entire league in scoring. The following season, he made All-League First Team and this time led the league in foul shooting. The year beginning in 1949 also resulted in his selection as All-League First Team as he placed fourth in league scoring. He retired in 1956, but returned ten years later as general manager and coach of the American Basketball Association's New York Nets.

Letter from Max Zaslofsky To This Author, Dated September 3, 1974

"A few years ago, on the National Basketball Association's twenty-fifth anniversary, I was selected along with 24 other players as the 25 best players in the NBA for the last 25 years."

(Photo courtesy of Max Zaslofsky)

TED KID LEWIS

Born Gershon Mendeloff but fighting under the name Ted Kid Lewis, this World Welterweight Champion held the title from 1915 through 1919. He created a rivalry with fellow welterweight Jack Britton that began with a no decision on March 26, 1915 and continued through February 7, 1921 with a 15-round loss to Britton. In all, the fighters engaged in 20 bouts—with Ted Kid Lewis winning three, Britton four, two draws, and 11 no decisions. The Lewis-Britton friction would go down in history as sports' most torrid rivalry—more fierce than the Yankees and Brooklyn Dodgers and more enduring than Muhammad Ali and Joe Frazier.

In Nat Fleischer's 1962 *Ring Record Book and Boxing Encyclopedia,* among all-time welterweights, he ranked Ted Kid Lewis number four—just behind Jack Britton. The Lewis-Britton friction endures forever.

According to Nat Fleischer, from the time Ted Kid Lewis began his ring career in 1910, he engaged in more than 400 battles. Although just five-foot-five-and-a-half and often as light as 126 pounds, Ted Kid Lewis fought many of those battles as a middleweight and against leading light heavyweight and heavyweight contenders.

MARILYN RAMENOFSKY

As an unheralded Maccabiah veteran in 1963, Marilyn Ramenofsky emerged at the top ranking of 400-meter women freestyle swimming. The next year she would break the world record three times—capturing an Olympic silver medal along the way. All of this culminated in her induction into the International Swimming Hall of Fame. In a letter to me dated June 21, 1973, International Swimming Hall of Fame Director Buck Dawson wrote this about Marilyn Ramenofsky: "She was the first female to swim a perfect freestyle stroke."

She has surfaced again here with another distinction—top placement among women in these Jewish-American All-Time Athletic Rankings and a seventeenth rank overall. In a letter to me dated December 19, 1973, Marilyn Ramenofsky wrote: "The true crisis of the Munich Olympics is its evolution away from the original intent of athletic competition. The modern games breed extreme nationalism, which results in the epitome of violent extremism."

After a graduate degree in insect neurondocrinology, she applied scuba diving to investigate the physiological effects of certain organic chemicals on marine crustacea.

Letter from Marilyn Ramenofsky, Dated December 19, 1973

"I have always felt that the Jewish community has backed my efforts and—as my career progressed—so did my Jewish following. Beginning in 1961, my family and the Phoenix Jewish community provided a great deal of spiritual support and helped raise travel money for my first international swimming competition as a member of the U.S. Maccabiah Team in Israel. In 1964, as the only Jewish woman on the U.S. Women's Olympic Swimming Team and a world record holder, I felt a strong Jewish sentiment both at home and abroad. This Jewish recognition was culminated for me upon my return to Israel for the 1965 Maccabiah Games. I was applauded as a champion by my competitors, by my teammates and by the people of Israel—what a wonderful memory! The great interest in and commitment to striving athletes stems from the pride Jews feel and place upon achievement in any field.

"I do not feel it is my obligation as a former world-class athlete to speak on the condition of world politics. Rather: it is my obligation as an informed woman, concerned human being and American Jew. Personally, I dislike the misuse of privileges and recognition that success in any endeavor provides for the promotion of selfish intentions. It is wrong to utilize athletic success as a stepping stone for political or theatrical careers. Each endeavor demands merit in its own right.

"While I was intensely training, I had very little time for extra things. The devotion to my sport was total. As a high school student: my life was filled with five to six hours of training a day, competition and studies. In a very real sense, the world-class athlete lives in a vacuum. Time is strictly portioned; the majority of that time is spent in the solitude of training. In 1964, I was not particularly politically aware and was in no position to serve as a political spokesman.

"My major concern was the blatant absence of collegiate swimming scholarships available to women. The situation forced me to confine my intensive training to the high school years; the same problem constrains many woman swimmers. It is one reason so many woman swimmers are so young.

"I don't interpret the Munich murders as a direct threat to American Jewish athletes, but rather as a threat to the fragile state of mankind. Stricter security measures could have been taken for the Israeli athletes and coaches in light of incidents prior to the tragedy. I feel greatly embittered. It was an acrimonious invasion of human

Marilyn Ramenofsky—the greatest Jewish-American woman athlete of all-time. (Photo courtesy of Marilyn Ramenofsky)

decency. It was particularly poignant for me, for I could vividly identify with the Jewish athletes and the environs of an Olympic village. But, the true crisis of the Munich killings is directly related to the nature of the modern Olympic Games and its evolution away from the original intent of athletic competition. Historically, the Olympics were a site where all political hostilities were diisplaced in favor of pure competition. However, the modern Games breed extreme nationalism, which results in the epitome of violent extremism.

"Munich did not just happen; there were intermediate steps that set the stage. I witnessed these intermediate steps. In the 1964 Olympic village at Tokyo: I recall official gold, silver and bronze medal tally boards posted in key sites throughout the village. The U.S. officials and coaches were extremely cognizant of winning gold medals and freely imparted their values to the athletes. Gold medal winners were given preferential treatment over other team members—such as an airplane trip to Osaka from Tokyo, while the other team members were dispatched by train.

"As a young athlete: this seemed alien to the ideals of the Olympic Games and to myself, in its underrating of the value of pure competition. Is placing first in an Olympic event the only significant accomplishment in an Olympic Games experience? Do only gold medals build human character? It seemed to me at the time that the U.S. had misplaced its priorities at expense of its youth.

"There were other inequalities indicating a departure from the original tenets of the Olympic Games. Medals are not awarded equally among all the sports; for example, there are many more medals given in swimming than in gymnastics. So, how can medal accumulation in a particular sport indicate national strength? Some South African countries preferentially select white athletes over black. National television networks greatly distort the overall view of the Games by televising only those sports in which Americans are winning. There exist too many inequalities in a facet of human existence where one would hope that all political gains and motives would be put aside. In comparison to Munich, events at Tokyo seem trivial. But, they are indicative of where priorities were being placed.

"The Munich tragedies of where priorities were poignantly indicative of the times and the evolution of attitudes away from the original designs of athletic competition. The supreme joy of the Olympics is meeting people from all over the world. You meet these people on a level where only one language is spoken: pure competition. My most cherished memories are of those times in the village when all athletes congregated to eat, socialize, bank, shop, dance, communicate and compete.

"But, these memories are riddled with the interventions of the American officials and coaches who were not in touch with American youth, but politically aligned. I felt that the personality of American youth was not being clearly represented by these American officials, who were caught up in the political importance of the Olympics and not particularly interested in international communication. Hopefully, with a new Olympic president: fresh energy will be acquired to implement positive changes in the format of international competition and communication. That would spell the end of the decaying process plaguing the modern Olympics. It would spell the end of the process setting the stage for Munich, 1972.

"In retrospect: I feel there was some prejudice shown against me by the U.S. Olympic Women's swimming coach and some preference was given to other swimmers on the team. Whether that was because I was Jewish, I cannot directly relate."

DICK SAVITT

At six-feet-three-inches, he towered over most of his tennis opponents. Power was his game; Savitt was his name. In 1951, Dick Savitt powered his way to the men's singles Wimbledon and Australia championships. But for some inexplicable reason, Dick Savitt was denied the opportunity to represent the United States in that year's Davis Cup Challenge Round—a round that would be lost by the United States with a loss that very possibly could have been averted if Savitt had not been bypassed. The following year, a bitter Dick Savitt retired. The story sounds as if it were a prelude to baseball piching star Ken Holtzman's League Championship and World Series benching while the New York Yankees went down to defeat 25 years before. Just as Savitt did, Ken Holtzman opted for a premature retirement in disgust. Savitt, however, did embark on a limited comeback.

The indomitable power behind his ground strokes presented a relentless attack that continually kept his opponents on the defensive. Without doubt, Dick Savitt was the greatest Jewish tennis player of all time.

NANCY LIEBERMAN

At some point between 1976 and 1980, Nancy Lieberman elevated women's collegiate basketball into a major competitive sport. A three-time All-America and two-time national Player of the Year, Lieberman led Old Dominion University to its first two women's national basketball championships scoring an average of more than 18 points per game and collecting almost nine rebounds per game. She also averaged more than seven assists per game. In the 1976 through 1977 academic year, she nearly averaged a triple double—with a scoring average of 20.9 points, an average of more than 10 rebounds per game, and almost eight assists per game. She was selected winner of the prestigious Broderick Cup, awarded annually to the top women's collegiate athlete in the country, and the Wade Trophy twice. In addition to being the youngest member of the 1976 Olympic team, Nancy Lieberman was the first woman to play in a men's professional summer league and in a National Basketball Association training camp. The Olympic silver medalist would go on to earn recognition as the greatest female basketball player ever.

In her 1982 book, *Basketball My Way* with Myrna and Harvey Frommer and published by Charles Scribner's Sons, Nancy Lieberman recalled that she was "an oddity for many—a girl playing in what had always been a male dominated sport." Then, she added: "I guess a little Jewish girl who dressed in cutoffs and had a comb stuffed in her back pocket with a wad of gum in her cheek was not your typical basketball player." She expressed pride in holding her own in competition with men in the 1980 New York Summer Professional League.

The five-foot-ten-inch Lieberman created mismatches in the backcourt as a guard, averaging around four steals a game. Against female competition, she was virtually unstoppable when attempting to score from inside. And against males, she held her own. But against the press, Nancy Lieberman endured an onslaught of vicious—and from all evidence absolutely false—innuendo and rumor about her personal life that was unprecedented in sports and without probable cause. In an apparent effort to come to her defense, a August 22, 1986 *USA Today* feature on Lieberman highlighted a statement from her on black basketball star Ralph Sampson that "Ralph and I are good friends . . . (who) can sit down and talk basketball." Five years earlier, many newspapers reported heavily on Lieberman's denial that she had a romance with female tennis star Martina Navratilova—another good platonic friend according to Navratilova herself. If the sensational spreading of totally false innuendo and rumor about her was a product of anti-Semitism, it is ironic; because Nancy Lieberman was among those who elected to keep her religious and political views private.

In the 1980 New York Summer Professional League, Lieberman would play in the same backcourt with the former men's professional All Star Nate "Tiny" Archibald. (Photo courtesy of Old Dominion University)

NANCY LIEBERMAN
5-11 GUARD
OLD DOMINION UNIVERSITY

STEVE STONE

In 1980, pitcher Steve Stone achieved the most difficult accomplishment in sports; he advanced from performing at a level considered good to sheer greatness. In 1980, Steve Stone won the American League Cy Young Award given annually to the best pitcher with a 25-win season that included 14 consecutive victories and a perfect outing in the All Star Game. It was a dream year. Then, he developed arm trouble and it was over—just like that. His own poetry, written as a student at Kent State University, became prophetic: "So you say you were the best today! . . . The glory was just borrowed and soon a guy will come to take it back. . . . So for today, kid you're the best—but remember without a break or two you'd have lost . . . The top of the world and the bottom aren't really that far apart—now are they?"

In a letter to me postmarked May 5, 1973, Steve Stone reflected upon his thoughts about the Munich murders and told me he didn't think Jewish athletes should be worried about entering pro-sports because of future terrorist incidents.

STEVE STONE

(Photo courtesy of the San Francisco Giants)

The strong-armed major league baseball pitcher showed flashes of brilliance in the seventies, but didn't have the staying power to advance beyond the limited role of spot starter. As a battery-mate of New York Yankee catching star Thurman Munson at Kent State University, Steve was selected team captain by his teammates and earned a berth on the All-Conference team. The articulate athlete would follow the tradition of many other Jews in sports by combining scholarly pursuits with physical accomplishment; several of Steve's poems would receive national publication.

Text of Letter from Steve Stone To This Author, Dated May 5, 1973

"The Munich tragedy was quite shocking as well as a black day for international athletics. There is no personal threat, so American Jewish athletes aren't given special protection. Any Jewish athlete scared away from professional sports either lacks the drive or the intestinal fortitude to make it anyway. We have a job to do and religion doesn't affect performance."

HAROLD SOLOMON

With excellent ground strokes and a tricky slice spin serve, Harold Solomon burst high into the top 10 rankings of professional tennis players in the seventies. His ability to retrieve would often wear down larger and more powerful opponents. With a style of frequent lobs and a two-handed backhand drive, he compensated for his lack of power and tendency not to employ drop shots with extraordinary accuracy. As a 20-year-old, Harold Solomon burst into stardom with what *Sports Illustrated* termed "the most crucial U.S. Davis Cup point in several years." At the time, he was the youngest player ever to represent the United States on the Davis Cup team.

In a letter to me dated July 10, 1973, Harold Solomon vividly described the incredible secrecy and extraordinary security surrounding his Davis Cup experiences in Romania as an aftermath of the Munich murders. The most shocking revelation was that he was never allowed to go in the same direction twice.

Text of Letter From Harold Solomon To This Author, Dated July 10, 1973

"I have received many letters from Jewish people throughout the world. From these letters: I have come to realize that I do have a rather large following in the Jewish population—especially in Europe. It is very satisfying to know that there are people following you who are also behind you all the way.

"It is difficult to say if Jewish athletes should step outside their field to comment on the various injustices that are heaped upon our people from day to day. An athlete must be careful, for he is, in effect, in the entertainment business and must always watch not to offend any large sector of the paying public.

"I was appalled at what took place in Munich; and there can never be any justification for actions that took place in Germany before that. Shortly after the Munich tragedy in Romania—during our Davis Cup match—Jewish athletes were forced to take very severe security precautions.

"The entire airfield was surrounded by soldiers with machine guns. The secret service came up to us immediately. We had private body guards, our own elevator in the hotel, an escape rope from our rooms, closed circuit television watching us, a motor van that wasn't allowed to stop and rules that we never went in the same direction twice.

"If terrorist activity is allowed to continue: I feel, in the years to come, it could pose a threat to Jewish athletes—both in Europe and in the United States. So far in my career, I have been quite fortunate in that I've encountered no overt prejudice or any form of discrimination.

"I have always had sports heroes in the different sports, but I have not picked one because of his being Jewish; I admire each athlete on his appeal and ability in his specialty. As far as my career is concerned: I have always wanted to be the best tennis player in the world and I will continue to strive for that goal; I feel it is a realistic goal. I plan to play tennis as long as I am able to compete on a level with my peers and still enjoy the game."

(Photo courtesy of the United States Tennis Lawn Association, by Russ Adams)

BATTLING LEVINSKY

November 6, 1918 would have been a landmark date in sports history if just one attempted haymaker had connected—one missed punch from the fist of Battling Levinsky striking the jaw of future World Heavyweight Champion Jack Dempsey, perhaps catching Dempsey off guard in a vulnerable moment. Battling Levinsky or perhaps even his real name of Barney Lebrowitz would be a modern-day household name. But in round three, the legendary Dempsey knocked Levinsky out. Still, the five-foot-eleven inch and 175 pound Battling Levinsky accomplished enough to prompt Nat Fleischer's rank of sixth greatest light heavyweight boxer of all time.

On October 24, 1916, Levinsky avenged an earlier loss by decision to Jack Dillon—the light heavyweight to whom Nat Fleischer gave the third all-time rank in his 1962 *Ring Record Book and Boxing Encyclopedia*—to win the World Lightweight Championship. Four years later, Levinsky lost the title to Georges Carpentier—Fleischer's seventh ranked light heavyweight of all time. Levinsky was some four inches taller and 15 pounds heavier than Daniel Mendoza, the first Jewish world champion—the World Heavyweight Champion between 1791 and 1795 during the developmental stages of professional boxing.

Beryl Lebrowitz a.k.a. Barney Williams a.k.a. Battling Levinsky. Set the all-time record for industry by fighting in three different localities on the same day.

ANDY COHEN

Two of the greatest players in history preceded Andy Cohen as 1928 second baseman of the New York Giants. Frankie Frisch and the recently traded Rogers Hornsby had elevated the fans' expectations for performance at that position to an unrealistically high level—a level that the solid Andy Cohen could never expect to approach. By coincidence, the Giants opened the 1928 campaign against Hornsby's new team. Cohen demonstrably outplayed Hornsby that day in winning the game for New York. When his unexpected hot hitting won the following Sunday game, Jewish fans mobbed Andy Cohen and carried him off the field. In his September 12, 1935 *Sporting News* article, Frederick G. Lieb recalled the enormous pressure thrust upon the 23-year-old Cohen: "Three newspapers were running his life story . . . He was asked . . . to come to this and that event, to help out this Jewish charity. He was losing a pound a day. Jewish admirers besieged his house, camped there day and night to get a peek at Andy. (Manager John) McGraw had to get him another residence and put him in hiding." Although he had compiled a respectable .281 batting average, within another year he was out of the Major Leagues forever.

In a letter to me postmarked June 21, 1973—when I had initially set out to establish a Jewish Sports Hall of Fame—Andy Cohen's brother reflected upon Andy's ordeal as well as his own brief pitching career with the Washington Nationals. This is how Syd Cohen—who surrendered Babe Ruth's last American League home run—before striking Ruth out in what would be his last American League at bat—remembered:

"There was prejudice, but I didn't have to take it. When someone would make a slur against Judaism or against Jewish people, I would tell them off. Many times my teammates said they'd back me up all the way; they knew how proud I was to be Jewish.

"Neither my brother, Andy, nor I ever played ball on either Rosh Hashanah or Yom Kippur. Our wonderful mother told us people would have more respect for Jews by our not working on these special days. At no time in history did Jewish greats of any sport ever work on the High Holy Days. Greenberg, Koufax, Holtzman and all the rest sat in the Synagogue and prayed.

"Jewish people are always glad to see a Jewish boy or girl engage in sports. Because of this, the Jewish athlete wants in the worst way to reach the top."

Earlier that month—in a letter to me postmarked June 8, 1973—Andy Cohen recalled how so many people looked upon him as a Great Jewish Hope. The Andy Cohen saga of a promising career cut short by the pressure of trying to fulfill impossible demands innocently set by an ethnic following has earned him a top quarter in these all-time athletic rankings.

Text of Letter From Andy Cohen To This Author, Dated June 8, 1973

"The label 'Great Jewish Hope' did inflict pressure. It did seem to spur me on, but as I look back: there were times I tried too hard. I certainly was aware of a special following from Jewish fans; I guess I considered myself a representative of these people.

"I encountered prejudice from players as well as fans. The tremendous publicity and the fact I played so well in my first game helped cause the prejudice. But: I had true friends in my manager, most of my teammates, several umpires and some of the reporters covering the club.

"Much of the publicity created good will. For the first time in its history, *Fourants*—the well-known Jewish paper—ran box scores of New York Giant baseball games. After an off-day at the Polo Grounds, the *Fourants* ran a banner on its front page that read: "No Game Today; Andy Must Be Sick."

"Many of the Jewish fans who came to the Polo Grounds for the first time asked what kind of seats were available. Ticket sellers would offer them box seats behind first or third base. Some of these fans would insist on box seats behind second base.

"All of the New York papers ran humorous cartoons about me. My favorite showed a Jewish mother urging her son to eat a certain brand of soup, 'So you will grow up to be like Andy C.'"

(Photo courtesy of Andy Cohen)

SID GORDON

In the forties and early fifties, he provided a consistently powerful bat to the New York Giants, Boston and Milwaukee Braves, and Pittsburgh Pirates—that is how major league baseball remembers Sid Gordon. In a given year, Gordon could be counted upon to contribute more than 20 to 30 home runs and nearly 100 runs batted in. Primarily an outfielder, he could play the infield adequately enough to fill in when necessary. Unlike many home run hitters, Sid Gordon also hit for average—generally above .280 because of his ability to avoid prolonged slumps.

Although he did not have the longevity of a latter-day Reggie Jackson—partially because of military service—or the grace of a Fred Lynn, he produced as much as either of these latter-day stars with the exception of spectacular starts in their first full seasons and one or two career years that made Jackson and Lynn bigger than life. Sid Gordon played his first full season of Major League Baseball in 1943. If just in that one year he had hit say 40 home runs—perhaps with the first 30 coming over the first half of that season—and then reverted to his actual production levels for the remainder of his career, more attention would have been focused upon him with higher expectations. When his career was over, the memory of anticipated greatness would have hyped his record as well.

BRIAN GOTTFRIED

Hard-hitting Brian Gottfried followed his serve to the net to add even more power to his returns. As a semifinalist in 1980, he came the closest of all Jewish players to Dick Savitt's Wimbledon championship—a championship won by Savitt the year before Brian Gottfried was born. Although he won a long list of tournaments, his most dramatic moment came in the United States Open 1976 quarterfinals when only a miracle rally by the legendary Bjorn Borg deprived Gottfried of what would have been a spectacular upset victory on national television. Over the years, he managed to defeat most of the big names of his era. He continually ranked in the top ten of all professional men's singles and doubles tennis players.

(Photo courtesy of the United States Tennis Lawn Association, by Russ Adams)

In a letter to me postmarked December 8, 1973, Brian Gottfried expressed a definitive opinion that sports and politics should be kept separate. "The two have very little in common and it takes a different type of person to do each," he pointed out.

But, Less than a decade-and-a-half later, two Jewish movie stars' criticism of Israel's forcefully resilient stand against violent Palestinians protesting Zionism proved that famous individuals removed from politics do indeed exert an enormous impact on public opinion. Woody Allen and Richard Dreyfuss received welcome coverage by a media that had been collectively critical of the Jewish State without the dilution of a rational justification for Israel's actions that could have been provided by a comparably prominent Jewish public figure outside of politics—such as a famous Jewish athlete.

Text of Letter from Brian Gottfried To This Author, Dated December 8, 1973

"On the tennis circuit: there are so many different nationalities represented, it is impossible to keep track of who comes from where, much less everybody's religion. The only people that really dwell on a person's background are the press. They seem to bring out the most insignificant details and characterize a person by them. I have never known a player that dislikes another player because of his background. It usually goes much deeper than that.

"I am also of the opinion that sports and politics should be kept separate. The two have very little in common and it takes a different type of person to do each. I thought the Mid-East conflict was handled well enough by Mr. Kissinger and didn't need me to help it along, because—as I said—I am a tennis player and not a politician.

"The only time I ever came across the threat of terrorism was in Romania at the 1972 Davis Cup and that wasn't much because we were so well protected that it never developed.

"I am proud of my heritage. But, I want to become the best tennis player in the world regardless of race, nationality or religion."

BARNEY ROSS

Unlike the modern era of multiple champions in subdivided weight classes, Barney Ross fought at a time in which there were single champions and wide variances between the weight limits of each division. Ross made the Boxing Hall of Fame in 1956 after a career in the thirties that produced three titles—World Lightweight Champion, World Junior Welterweight Champion, and World Welterweight Champion. In his 1962 *Ring Record Book and Boxing Encyclopedia,* Nat Fleischer ranked Ross as the ninth best welterweight of all-time. He held the lightweight and junior welterweight titles simultaneously. Although Ross only made Nat Fleischer's rankings as a welterweight, it was the seventh ranked all-time lightweight that Ross beat for that title; and he did it twice.

A movie depicting Barney Ross's life dramatized the impact that the dramatic death of his father, resultant poverty, bad company, heavy war combat, and related drug addiction exerted. Born Barnet Rosofsky, he fought under the name Barney Ross to conceal his boxing from his mother. Little did either of them know that name would be remembered forever.

(Photo courtesy of Barney Ross)

JULIE HELDMAN

Julie Heldman was born to play tennis. Her father won singles titles in several levels of competition, her mother played at Wimbledon before going on to introduce a major tennis magazine, and a younger sister also won numerous tournaments. Her vast experience enabled her to use the entire court to frustrate opponents, who would frequently tire from the added running. Generally ranked high in the top ten, Heldman gained prominence by wearing down Billie Jean King with her patented style of spraying the ball throughout the entire court and forcing King to surrender after King's heralded victory over Bobby Riggs. But, her greatest achievement had come in 1969 when she won the Italian Open. After winning numerous tournaments, injuries caught up with Heldman. She later surfaced as a network tennis commentator.

(Photo courtesy of the United States Tennis Lawn Association, by Russ Adams)

BRAD GILBERT

From a tennis standpoint, his victories over John McEnroe and Jimmy Connors might mean more; however in 1987, Brad Gilbert scored a victory on the tennis court that has monumental importance from a historical standpoint. He defeated former Wimbledon champion, Boris Becker—a German with an enormous following from his homeland. By virtue of his age and gentlemanly demeanor, Becker had no involvement with or even vague resemblance to the monsters from his country who had murdered six million Jews. But, he had emerged as the first national German sports hero since the former World Heavyweight Boxing Champion Max Schmeling—who served as a paratrooper with the German Army during the Holocaust. If the match between Gilbert and Becker had taken place fifty years earlier, it would have attracted the same intense support as that afforded the 1936 fight between Schmeling and Joe Louis in which Louis annihilated Schmeling much to the chagrin of Adolf Hitler. The very fact that—after Germany's all-out effort to rid the world of Jewish people—a Jewish person stepped up and defeated the greatest German athlete in 50 years demonstrated that the Holocaust had failed.

One of the fastest players on the circuit—Brad Gilbert had arrived.

Although Brad Gilbert never expressed any feelings of religious significance to his victory over Boris Becker, I did find one prominent tennis star who had definitive opinions on the subject in 1974 when I interviewed her. Only a chronic back ailment prevented Nancy Ornstein from climbing to among the top-ranked women tennis players in the world; at one time or another, she had beaten many of them. The counterpunching Ornstein depended on ground strokes and running away from the net to become Middle Atlantic Women's Champion in that year. As a teenager, she had been ranked as high as fourth in the nation at that level. This is what she had to say:

"I would love playing in Germany, but I feel a certain coldness from the German people. One time I played a German I felt as if it were German against Jew, rather than just a tennis match. I normally evaluate people as individuals, but it is hard to forget the past.

"I think Jewish people should stick together as a family. The Jewish athlete lucky enough to have influence should use it to our advantage, especially for causes important to Jewish people. Winning tennis tournaments means receiving great letters from Jewish people; we are proud of our successful athletes.

"I felt the threat of terrorism in London at Heathrow Airport, which had tanks surrounding it. There had been articles about Arab terrorists blowing up airports, with Jews as targets. I was realy frightened.

"The only open prejudice I came against was in the Philadelphia area."

On February 24, 1988—some 14 years after my first interview with Ornstein—she confirmed that she still felt the same way. But, with respect to Brad Gilbert's victory over Boris Becker, she said: "I consider Boris a wonderful human being, so I felt no special satisfaction in his defeat."

Many athletes of Jewish heritage find themselves having to publicly decide how they personally wish to acknowledge the Holocaust. In a letter postmarked in August 1974, former New York Cosmos soccer player Roby Young expressed his opinion: "Whether to play in Germany or not is a long-term argument in Israel. My feelings are that we should play there in order to prove that the nation of Israel is alive. Yet, we should never forget what their parents have done to our nation and to the world. I would play there and try to play my best ever!!"

In 1987, Brad Gilbert defeated Boris Becker not once, but three times; he also helped the United States reach the World Team Cup finals in Dusseldorf, West Germany. Two of Brad Gilbert's greatest achievements came in 1985 and 1986 with tournament championships in Tel Aviv, Israel.

THE JEWISH-AMERICAN ALL-TIME ATHLETIC RANKINGS

The Second Great Jewish Twenty-Eight

29. Peter Revson
30. Louis Kid Kaplan
31. Roby Young
32. Harry Newman
33. Tom Okker
34. Buddy Myer
35. Erskine Mayer
36. George Stone
37. Shep Messing
38. Ed Reulbach
39. Marshall Goldberg
40. Randy Grossman
41. Albert Schwartz
42. Lou Gordon
43. Max Baer
44. Art Heyman
45. Harry Danning
46. Larry Sherry
47. Phil Weintraub

48. Mike Rossman

49. Benny Kauff

50. Sonny Hertzberg

51. Goody Rosen

(tie) 52.   Marty Fleckman

(tie) 52.   Aaron Krickstein

(tie) 53.   Martin Jaite

(tie) 53.   Eadie Wetzel

(tie) 54.   Steve Tannen

(tie) 54.   Eliot Teltscher

55. Amos Mansdorf

56. Norman Sper, Jr.

PETER REVSON

Without question, the most controversial selection to the Jewish Sports Hall of Fame and placement in the Jewish-American All-Time Athletic Rankings has to be Peter Revson. In 1974, he was reported to be universally "acknowledged as the leading road racing driver in the United States and one of the foremost drivers in the world" in a wire release from United Press International on March 22—the day Peter Revson died. But his mother was not Jewish; and he did not practice the religion. His tragically untimely death had nothing to do with this induction. Peter Revson earned this distinction for his athletic brilliance coupled with his Jewish heritage and a process of elimination among two established and substantially prominent race car drivers who met the traditional criteria of having Jewish mothers.

I initially set out to establish the Jewish Sports Hall of Fame in the spring of 1973 with an objective in including competitors from all major sports. One contender for inclusion as a race car driver was Steve Krisiloff, who had placed sixth in prize money in the 1973 Indianapolis 500-mile race. In a remarkable letter to me postmarked October 29, 1973, his father—Mike Krisiloff—pulled his son out of contention: "I have not previously responded to your letter because I thought your project would fade away like a bad dream. It's funny, but I don't recall any books about Catholic athletes,

(In car): Courtesy of Indianapolis Motor Speedway Corporation

or Protestant ones, or even any Baptists. Mario Andretti is a Catholic, but I never see any mention of that fact when he wins a race. What is A. J. Foyt's religion? Or the Unsers'? We are proud to be Jews, but I think your book is in bad taste."

The obvious response to that opinion is that the prominence of Jewish people in the arts and sciences once indisputably cast a weakling Jewish stereotype. The Jew in American sports has changed that perception. His or her physical prowess has come to be seen as a trait identified with Jews in general. Had Steve Krisiloff carved a mark in his sport as indelible as Sandy Koufax or Mark Spitz did—for historical accuracy—I would have included him anyway.

In the early seventies, South African Jody Scheckter won or finished high in several major races. He became the second driver to have an opportunity to compete in the nationally televised Super Star Sports Tournament that Peter Revson had nearly won in what would have been a stunning upset the year before. But, in a letter dated September 9, 1974, Jody Scheckter's manager Nick Brittan wrote: "Regarding your Jewish-American Sports Hall of Fame: For reasons connected with Mr. Scheckter's personal security, we seek to avoid potential acts of terrorism by not publicizing the fact that he is Jewish. We must therefore formally insist that no mention of him is made in your forthcoming book." Here, I had set out to establish a Jewish Sports Hall of Fame as a memorial to the eleven slain Israeli athletes at the Munich Olympics; if the result stood to endanger—or even to inconvenience—any of the athletes I intended to honor by magnifying them as a target for anti-Semitic aggression, even the benefit of promoting Jewish athletic prowess could not justify that risk. Within 24 hours of receiving this letter, I made the announcement that I was suspending my efforts to establish a Jewish Sports Hall of Fame.

In 1979, through a totally unrelated effort, a Jewish Sports Hall of Fame was founded at the Wingate Institute for Physical Education and Sport, in Netanya, Israel. Ironically—some four years later—Jody Scheckter was inducted. Until then, the only comprehensive published work that identified Jewish athletes was Bloch Publishing Company's 1965 *Encyclopedia of Jews in Sports* by Bernard Postal, Jesse Silver, and Roy Silver—which was published before Jody Scheckter began his racing career and enough years out of date not to draw attention to athletes or former athletes who were listed. But that year—1983—JD Publishers, Inc. released a compendium of biographical sketches entitled *Great Jews in Sports,* by Robert Slater, which did publicize the fact that Jody Scheckter was Jewish. With that information in the public's domain and other athletes annually being inducted into the Jewish Sports hall of Fame in Israel, I resumed this work—again focusing on auto racing for successful representatives to include.

It was then that I turned to a letter addressed to me with a postmark of May 16, 1973. It was from Peter Revson. When I initially contacted him, I was unaware that his mother was not Jewish. But, Peter Revson welcomed my consideration of him for inclusion in the Jewish Sports Hall of Fame and expressed pride in his Jewish heritage. Peter Revson is my selection for twenty-ninth place on the Jewish-American All-Time Athletic Rankings in the Jewish Sports Hall of Fame. Peter would have liked that. Although just half-Jewish, Peter Revson took pride in identifying with Jewish causes. Peter Revson was handsome, affluent, unpretentious, and gifted—so gifted he stunned the sports world by nearly winning the first Super Star Sports tournament. He was linked romantically with the then Miss World, but his biggest love was with racing cars. Acknowledged as the leading road racing driver in the nation and one of the greatest drivers in the world, Peter won both the British and Canadian Grand Prix in 1973. But, his greatest racing year was 1971—the year he won the pole position in the

Indianapolis 500 for U.S. Auto Club Championship cars with a record 178.696 an hour and finished the race as runner-up. Peter Revson's younger brother had died in a 1967 racing accident; his parents wanted him to quit. There was evidence Peter wanted to quit, after just a few more races. I talked with Peter Revson about religion and life. Then Peter's car would burst into flames in South Africa and it was all over.

Text of Letter from Peter Revson To This Author, Dated May 16, 1973

"I was angered as much as anyone could have been regarding Munich. However, I see it more as part of the conflict between warning factions than as nonpolitical racial violence. My mother is a WASP. But, being half-Jewish, I am very sympathetic and understanding of Jewish problems.

"I have encountered very little prejudice on account of my ethnic background. If I do encounter it, I put myself in a position where I don't have to tolerate it."

LOUIS KID KAPLAN

The date was January 2, 1925. The place was Madison Square Garden in New York. With more than 14,000 spectators in attendance, Louis Kid Kaplan knocked Danny Kramer down and out in the ninth round to win the World Featherweight Championship—which would some day earn him distinction by boxing authority Nat Fleischer as the tenth greatest featherweight of all time in his 1962 *Ring Record Book and Boxing Encyclopedia*. Two years later, he would eat his way out of the featherweight division and had to forfeit his title. In addition to his physical prowess, the name Kid Kaplan would become famous for sportsmanship and integrity after it became common knowledge that Kaplan, late in his career, had rejected a reported $50,000 to throw a fight.

Photo by Ring Magazine

ROBY YOUNG

Although ranked ahead of highly regarded goalie Shep Messing as the greatest Jewish soccer player to perform for an American team, forward Reuben Young never emerged as an all-time Jewish-American great; recurring leg injuries constrained the former Israeli Olympic team captain's speed and accuracy. Roby would return to Israel as a member of the Haboel football club. In a letter to me postmarked in August, 1974, Roby Young reflected upon Jews in sports:

Text of Letter from Roby Young To This Author, Dated August 1, 1974

"I think Jewish athletes should use their prominence to exert influence on public opinion and to change any image of an unathletic Jew. The unathletic image no longer exists, however, because of the influence of the State of Israel—with its young and strong generation.

"The people of Israel have learned to live with the threat of terrorism and to fight it. I feel the threat when terrorists succeed in their missions.

"I—as every man in Israel—am a soldier; but, since I already served two-and-one-half years in the army, I only serve about 60 days a year on reserve. The rest of the time, of course, I am subject to call.

"My greatest sports accomplishment was to represent Israel in the Olympic Games at Mexico in 1968 and to serve as the captain of the National Soccer Team for three years.

"Whether to play in Germany or not is a long-term argument in Israel. My feelings are that we shoud play there in order to prove that the Nation of Israel is alive. Yet, we should never forget what their parents have done to our nation and to the world. I would play there and try to play my best ever!!

"I never had a chance to play in Russia; Israel played Russia in 1956 at Moscow. I would play there for one reason: to lift the morale of the Jews of Russia. The Israeli flag and the National Anthem in the stadium would do it.

"I wish I could live to see a world without politics; I'd like a world of sports."

In a letter to me postmarked August 12, 1974, New York Cosmos Director of Sales Stephen Marshall rated Roby Young—shown here as he dribbles—as the best Jewish soccer player in the United States. "Our coach did not think Steve Greenberg could have made the Cosmos team," he noted. Then, he added: "In order of skills, I rate Roby Young, Shep Messing, and Steve Greenberg. None of these players would be considered an all-time great soccer player." (Photo courtesy of the New York Cosmos' by Paul Bereswill)

HARRY NEWMAN

An All-America football quarterback at the University of Michigan in the thirties, Harry Newman had a brief but spectacular professional career with the New York Giants. As a rookie in 1933, he guided the Giants to their first National Football League Championship game and almost won it with a sensational 13 consecutive completions. After a game in which he ran for more than 100 yards the following year, he suffered a near-crippling injury that ended the super quarterback's career nearly as dramatically as it had began. In a letter to me postmarked September 27, 1974, Minnesota Viking President Max Winter put Newman in the same class with the legendary quarterbacks Sid Luckman and Benny Friedman. Winter wrote: "It is unfair for me to rank them even though it was fortunate to see them all on several occasions. All three of them were very great quarterbacks and perhaps given the same chance to play on the same teams, I doubt that there could be a great comparison."

TOM OKKER

Tom Okker—as with Johnny Kling, Peter Revson, and Ed Reulbach—transcends the traditional criterion of having a Jewish mother for being considered Jewish. With the exception of Revson, inclusion in the Jewish Sports Hall of Fame honors those successful athletes with whom the public can associate their Jewish heritage. Associating a successful individual with a given group tends to perceptually transfer that success to the collective image of the group. Occasionally, the public scrutiny of famous individuals fails to reveal something as provocative as a Jewish heritage—in which case, the individual's success does not contribute to the public's continually formulating image of Jewish people in general. Such was the case of professional basketball star Rudy LaRusso, who played for the Los Angeles Lakers in the early sixties. In 1973, I was unable to obtain confirmation from LaRusso regarding whether published reports of his mother being Jewish were true. In a letter to me dated May 29, 1973, Los Angeles Lakers' publicity director Jeff Temkin wrote that to the best of his knowledge, "Rudy LaRusso is not Jewish, but Italian." In a letter to me dated June 8, 1973, from Dartmouth College—where LaRusso played—sports information director Jack DeGange indicated that he did not know, but directed me to a former teammate and close friend of LaRusso's and to the widow of his college coach. On the other hand, the public's association of Tom Okker with Judaism was so evident in 1973, that I was sent his photographs for my Jewish Sports Hall of Fame by the United States Lawn Tennis Association along with those of Harold Solomon, Brian Gottfried, and Julie Heldman that I had requested. In response to every inquiry on the subject, I was advised that Tom Okker encouraged the understanding that he was indeed Jewish. The fact that his mother was not of that faith has not diminished the transfer of the public's perception of his athletic ability to the collective image of Jewish people.

Tom Okker was nicknamed the Flying Dutchman for his amazing speed and quickness. He burst into stardom as a finalist in the 1968 United States Open and won the South African Title in 1968 and 1969. In the late seventies, he reached both the semifinals and quarterfinals at Wimbledon in successive years. As a doubles partner, he won the United States, Italian, and French Opens. He has indeed earned a place in the Jewish Sports Hall of Fame.

Tom Okker readily associated himself with his father's Judaism and emerged on the circuit as another of the fine line of Jewish tennis stars.

BUDDY MYER

After compiling a better than .300 lifetime batting average over 15 years primarily as a second baseman for the Washington Nationals, Buddy Myer joined a growing list of uninducted Jewish Hall of Fame candidates with a legitimate claim for entrance. In 1935, he led the league in batting with a .349 average and drove in 100 runs—an amazing figure for a second baseman, especially on a team without many other dangerous hitters. That same year, he also established a major league record for doubleplays by a second baseman. In his September 12, 1935 *Sporting News* article, Frederick G. Lieb wrote this about Buddy Myer: "Next to Greenberg among the Jewish ball players of all time, we must rank Charles Solomon (Buddy) Myer . . . He always has been a hard and aggressive player and good hitter."

ERSKINE MAYER

Although he pitched in the so-called dead ball era—an era in which league home run leaders averaged barely more than 10 per year and pitching earned run average leaders averaged less than three runs per nine innings—Erskine Mayer earns thirty-fifth place in the Jewish-American All-Time Athletic Rankings for having put together consecutive 20 win seasons and recording more wins than losses and an average of less than three earned runs per nine innings over his career. The right-handed Mayer relied upon an unorthodox delivery, spinning curve ball, and pinpoint control with sufficient speed to keep batters repeatedly off balance by varying it. In modern times, when quality pitchers became specialists for late inning relief work, Mayer might have achieved even greater stardom coming out of the bullpen.

Mayer escaped involvement with the 1919 Chicago White Sox's Black Sox Scandal as a teammate of Shoeless—"Say it ain't so, Joe"—Jackson and others who conspired to fix a World Series. He had spent 1912 through much of 1918 with the Philadelphia Phillies. He also roomed with Grover Cleveland Alexander—who would later be portrayed in a movie by actor Ronald Reagan.

GEORGE STONE

George Stone was one of the first bad-looking good hitters in baseball. Although his career was brief—between 1905 and 1910—he captured an American League batting title with a .358 average in 1906 and followed that season with a .320 mark. His left-handed stance was geared to go the other way—to left field. He thrived on making contact with slashing line drives to left center in the alley, bloop hits down the left field line, and bounding ground balls up the middle. He seldom struck out, but rarely pulled the ball either. Stone's excellent speed enabled him to steal as many as 35 bases in one year. But, his unorthodox batting stance limited his ability to beat out infield hits. In the late fifties and early sixties, the St. Louis Cardinals had a first baseman who hit very similar to Stone—who, by coincidence, played in St. Louis for the Browns. The Cardinals' first baseman's name was Joe Cunningham; and one year he hit .345 with the same bad-looking batting stance made famous by George Stone.

SHEP MESSING

He started as a two-time All-America soccer goalie at Harvard, Most Valuable Player of the NCAA finals in the Orange Bowl, member of the 1971 United States team during the Pan-American games, and goalkeeper of the United States Olympic team in 1972 at Munich.

When Messing joined the New York Cosmos, he brought with him a reputation for beiing flamboyant and controversial. He was remembered by his college teammates as the player who brought his pet boa constrictor to practice.

(Photo courtesy of New York Cosmos)

ED REULBACH

Ed Reulbach's accomplishments of compiling league-leading pitching records for three consecutive seasons and hurling shutouts in both games of a double-header on September 26, 1908, would normally warrant high ranking in the Jewish Sports Hall of Fame—except, according to a trainer quoted in Bloch Publishing Company's 1965 *Encyclopedia of Jews in Sports,* that day was a Jewish holiday—which diminishes the accomplishment because it was bound to be Rosh Hashanah or Yom Kippur by virtue of the date—and Ruelbach's Jewish heritage was only of an unspecified part that the trainer indicated he learned about sometime later. Further questions regarding whether Ed Reulbach was Jewish surface upon realization that Reulbach's name was not included in Frederick G. Lieb's September 12, 1935 *Sporting News* article, which provided an otherwise comprehensive review to that date, or National Baseball Hall of Fame Director Ken Smith's partial listing of old timers in his letter to me of May 22, 1973. Reulbach was cited as being Jewish in the JD Publishers, Inc. 1983 book, *Great Jews in Sports,* and in Shapolsky Publishers' 1987 book, *The Jewish Baseball Hall of Fame.* But, one thing is certain—Ed Reulbach was a top pitcher.

Reulbach compiled league leading records of 19–4 in 1906, 17–4 in 1907, and 24–7 in 1908 and a career earned run average of 2.28.

MARSHALL GOLDBERG

In the thirties, Marshall Goldberg gained fame as a two-time All America—one year at halfback and the next at fullback. At either position and as a kickoff returner, Goldberg was a breakaway threat with the potential to go all the way.

As a professional in the forties, Goldberg had the misfortune of playing with the Chicago Cardinals—a team with a perennially losing record brought about by an inadequate offensive line to support a running attack. So, Marshall Goldberg was forced to focus his contributions on defense. As a defensive back, he was able to utilize the speed that had made him a great college running back. At various times, he led the National Football League in interceptions and kickoff return average.

In a letter to me postmarked August 12, 1974, Goldberg indicated that he no longer thought about his athletic past: "I am too engrossed in my present activities to think about history."

Text of Letter From Marshall Goldberg To This Author, Dated August 12, 1974

"I am too engrossed in my present activities to think about history. Almost everything that I have thought about sports has been said and printed and I doubt that any additional views of mine would be of any importance.

"My place in American sports was created many years ago and the final chapter was written in 1948. I really have nothing pertinent to add."

RANDY GROSSMAN

In the National Football League strike year or 1974, Randy Grossman was one of five free agents to make the Pittsburgh Steelers. Little did he know that during his stay he would accumulate four Super Bowl rings. He scored the first Steeler touchdown in Super Bowl X against the Dallas Cowboys in 1975 after catching four critical passes in the American Football Conference Championship game. In 1978, he caught 37 passes for 448 yards and the following year averaged 18.1 yards per catch. His best single game performance came on October 23, 1978, when he caught nine passes against the Houston Oilers. But his longest reception came the following year against the Denver Broncos for a gain of 54 yards. Grossman was a reliable role player on what many consider to be the second greatest football dynasty to Vince Lombardi's Green Bay Packers.

Some considered Randy Grossman emerged as quarterback Terry Bradshaw's favorite receiver in short yard situations. (Photo courtesy of the Pittsburgh Steelers).

ALBERT SCHWARTZ

In 1930, Albert Schwartz moved into the limelight as a National Collegiate Athletic Association triple crown winner in freestyle swimming. The United States National Champion the next year for 100-yard freestyle, he would win an Olympic bronze medal in that category in 1932. He was later inducted into the International Swimming Hall of Fame.

Albert Schwartz was the United States National Champion in 1931 for the 100-yard freestyle and a frequent NCAA champion from Northwestern in the 50 and 100 free. (Photo courtesy of the International Swimming Hall of Fame)

LOU GORDON

A consensus All-America tackle in college, Lou Gordon kicked around several professional football teams before landing on a winner—the 1936 World Champion Green Bay Packers. Although his pro career didn't bring him the glory his college years did, Louis James Gordon had his moments—including a crucial fumble recovery in the

Packers' Championship-winning game. By 1930 standards, Lou Gordon was a bruising lineman—at more than 250 pounds. In a letter to me postmarked July 12, 1973, Lou Gordon explained that he did experience prejudice during his Freshman year of college.

Text of Letter From Lou Gordon To This Author, Dated July 12, 1973

"I was not necessarily aware of any special following from Jewish fans. I considered myself as an individual player and felt no obligation to stand up and act as a representative for the fans in matters of social interest.

"As a freshman football player at the University of Illinois, I encountered some prejudice. My religion did not play a factor in my career."

(Photo courtesy of Lou Gordon)

MAX BAER

Jews longed for one of their own to get in the boxing ring with Hitler's favorite boxer, Max Schmeling—whose promoter, to the shame of Jews everywhere, was Jewish. But, there just weren't any Jewish heavyweight boxers around. All of a sudden, a promising young heavyweight with an alleged Jewish strain in his family tree proclaimed himself Jewish. In 1934—with a Mogen David proudly on his trunks—

Photo by Jack Silver

Max Baer, would win the World's Heavyweight Boxing Championship. But June 8, 1933, was the night Maxie earned a spot in The Jewish Sports Hall of Fame. For nine rounds, he punched a bloody Max Schmeling around the ring; in round 10, Max Baer knocked Max Schmeling down and out. "It's round 10. Schmeling is covered with blood. Schmeling runs. The Jewish heavyweight is cracking lefts and rights to Schmeling's chin. The man from Germany is DOWN. It's all over!"

Had Max Baer actually been verifiably Jewish, he would have placed in the Jewish Second Superlative Seven rather than in the middle of the Second Great Jewish Twenty-Eight. While he did not dominate the heavyweight division with the devastating reign of the modern champion Mike Tyson, he may have been a better fighter than Tyson. In Baer's era, team sports paid lower salaries and offered less adulation than did boxing. In the modern era, large young men who demonstrate the rare combination of power and speed are directed into the more certain careers of football, basketball, or baseball. If the best athletes among big men—the Ron Mixes, Lawrence Taylors, Larry Birds, and Bo Jacksons—had been directed into boxing, as they might have been during the Max Baer era, it is possible that Mike Tyson would not be a household name.

ART HEYMAN

He was awesome in college and—as a Jewish scoring machine—a dream draft choice for the New York Knicks. But, against the larger opposition in the National Basketball Association, Art Heyman was unable to live up to expectations. Heyman had been selected NCAA Player of the Year in 1963 after three years of All-America status. He averaged 25.1 points per game over those three years. Heyman literally carried the Duke Blue Devils to the NCAA final four in 1963 and was named Most Valuable Player of the finals. But, his greatest performance came in dramatic fashion—in his 1963 regular season finale, where Heyman scored 40 points and pulled down 24 rebounds against arch-rival North Carolina. His six-season professional career included service with a number of teams in both the National Basketball Association and the then upstart American Basketball Association with scoring averages that ranged from the mid to high teens.

At six feet-five-inches, Art Heyman lacked the size to fully exploit his power scoring drive in the pros. He was virtually unstoppable in the college ranks. Along with David Thompson and perhaps Michael Jordan—both of whom came along later and enjoyed more successful professional careers—Heyman delivered the most dominant performances ever seen in the Atlantic Coast Conference for over a three-year period. (Photo courtesy of Duke University)

HARRY DANNING

For nearly a decade beginning in 1933, New York Giants catcher Harry Danning stood as one of baseball's best. The three-time All Star was the greatest catcher ever among Jews who played that position—unless the apparent myth that Johnny Kling had Jewish parents is actually true. Danning compiled a respectable .285 batting average over his career. But, he is best remembered for a few games in which he played on the level of a Greenberg or Ruth. On October 9, 1937, against the Yankees at the Polo Grounds in the fourth game of the World Series, Harry Danning emerged as hero of the game with a double, two singles, and two runs batted in as the Giants won. Earlier in that year, Danning stroked five hits in a single game. In a game during 1940, Harry Danning hit for the cycle—with a single, double, triple, and home run.

LARRY SHERRY

Hero of the 1959 World Series—from which he would become the first relief pitcher to be named Most Valuable Player—Larry Sherry provided inspiration for both Jewish and handicapped followers. Sherry was born with both feet deformed. But, he would play a vital part in changing the complexion of Major League Baseball as teams began to specialize some of their best pitchers in relief. Eventually, relief pitchers would virtually rule the sport and command the highest salaries. His brother Norm—a reserve catcher—provided the Los Angeles Dodgers with a brother pitching battery in the early sixties.

In the 1959 World Series, Los Angeles Dodger Larry Sherry came on in relief against the Chicago White Sox and repeatedly shut the door—with two victories and two saves, emerging as the hero in each one of the World Champion Dodgers' wins. (Photo courtesy of the Los Angeles Dodgers)

PHIL WEINTRAUB

A near .300 hitter from 1933 through 1945, Phil Weintraub alternated between first base and the outfield for the New York Giants primarily with interrupting stints on the Cincinnati Reds and Philadelphia Phillies. In Frederick G. Lieb's September 12, 1935 *Sporting News* article on Jewish baseball players, Lieb had Phil Weintraub patrolling centerfield for his mythical Jewish All-Star team comprised of former and active players to that date. More than half a century later, Weintraub would still have a place on that team.

MIKE ROSSMAN

Excluding bantamweight titles won by two Algerian Jews in the fifties, it had been approximately forty years since a Jewish fighter had won a world's championship. But, in 1978, Victor Galindez was hurt on national television; blood poured down his face.

The Jewish Bomber, shown here, four years before he would become World Boxing Association Light Heavyweight Champion, personified the great Jewish fighters of old. (Photo courtesy of Capital Centre)

His opponent was all over him. The referee stopped the fight and Mike Rossman—The Jewish Bomber, fighting with the Star of David on his trunks and under his mother's Jewish name—was the World Boxing Association Light Heavyweight Champion. Early in his career, as an undefeatd middleweight, Rossman had been the first Jewish fighter in years to fight at the fabled Madison Square Garden. After that fight, a mob of Jewish youths in yarmulkes would storm the Jewish Bomber's victorious locker room. During the fight, Rossman had received an unheard-of two standing ovations from the partisan Jewish crowd. In a letter to me, postmarked August 26, 1974, Mike Rossman reflected upon the significance of his being a Jewish fighter.

Text of Letter From Mike Rossman To This Author, Dated August 26, 1974

"I am in sports and not in politics. I am glad I was not around to meet Max Schmelling, for today I would be an old man. He may have knocked me out, because he was a good fighter.

"I am not bitter against anyone. Boxing is a sport to me. There are many promoters asking for me. They are all out to make money as there isn't or hasn't been a good Jewish fighter for a long time. Of course, I am making money too.

"I do like the sport. Many Jewish people—young and old—come to see me. This makes me work harder. I want to make them proud of me.

"I may go to Germany to fight next year and only to fight, not in anger about anything. I have received many letters from German Jews telling me they have read about me in the papers. They hope to see me fight one day in Germany."

BENNY KAUFF

At the age of 29, Benny Kauff had a career batting average of .311 in service with several baseball clubs between 1912 and 1920 with seemingly half a career ahead of him. In addition to his hitting, Kauff put fear into opposing clubs as one of the most prolific base stealers of his time. In the years ahead, Benny Kauff seemed destined for greatness—perhaps even a .400 batting average on his way to the National Baseball Hall of Fame—which, of course, was not in existence at that time. But, it was not to be. In 1920, Major League Baseball Commissioner K.M. Landis barred Benny Kauff permanently from the game. Kauff had been charged with larceny, but was acquitted. In spite of the fact that Kauff was found innocent, Landis took his unprecedented action. It would be the only time in baseball history that a player would be expelled without misconduct. Landis attributed his decision to Kauff's alleged association with so-called undesirable persons.

SONNY HERTZBERG

Sonny Hertzberg played professional basketball with New York in the 1947–48 campaign, Washington in 1948–49, and Boston in 1950–51. Selected All-Met at Tilden High School in 1939, he gained the same distinction at New York's City College in 1941 and 1942—when his team reached the semi-final round of the 1942 National Invitation Tournament in Madison Square Garden. As a professional, he gained fame for setting the single game scoring record with 37 points. In a letter to me postmarked September 3, 1974, Sonny Hertzberg described his playing assets. In his own words, Hertzberg cited "an accurate set shot" and his skill as a "play developer and strategist."

Four years of holocaust-era military service cut short Sonny Hertzberg's brilliant basketball career. The City College of New York Hall-of-Famer was captain and high scorer of the original Knickerboker and last Washington Capitols teams. After retirement, Hertzberg returned to New York to the Kinckerbockers for a scouting and radio and television commentary. He was a member of the B'nai B'rith Sports Lodge.

(Photo courtesy of Sonny Hertzberg)

SOME

PHOTOGRAPHS

OF

THE JEWISH

HALL OF FAME

ATHLETES

MIKE EPSTEIN   1B

In his 1973 book, *Kiss It Good-bye,* former Washington Senator announcer, Shelby Whitfield, had this to say about Mike Epstein: "Epstein took pleasure in looking down on the other players and placing himself on an intellectual pedestal. He was addicted to using big words." He emerged as a hero in 1972 by risking his life with Ken Holtzman and Richie Scheinblum in protesting that year's Munich murders of the Israeli Olympic Team by Arab terrorists.

(Courtesy of the California Angels)

MARSHALL GOLDBERG

A two-time All-American - - one year as a halfback and the next
as a fullback. He played for the Chicago Cardinals. See page 111.

(Photo courtesy of the University of Tennessee)

Ernie Grunfeld, while at the University of Tennessee, prior to his career with the New York Knicks. See page 166.

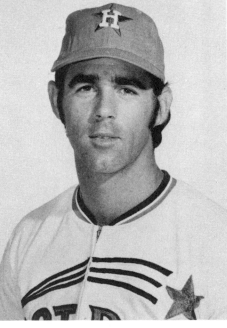

An acrobatically spectacular defensive outfielder, Norm Miller also posed a dangerous threat as a pinch hitter-- batting .323 in that capacity in 1973. (Photo courtesy of the Houston Astros)

Ken Holtzman and the Israeli National Basketball team, with coach Avraham Hemmo, shown dressed without the tie. Hemmo recalled how Holtzman and other Jewish American athletes took the risk of making themselves into additional targets for terrorism by publically protesting the Munich murders. "We were aware Holtzman and the other Jewish American athletes felt for their brothers who died in Munich." Hemmo said. (Photo courtesy of A.Hemmo)

(Photo courtesy of the Cincinnati Reds)

Richie Sheinblum, led the American League in hitting for most of 1972. See page 162.

Many consider Ron Mix to have been the greatest offensive lineman in professional football history. No other position of any sport requires the incumbent to react as quickly, hit as hard, and bear as much repetitive punishment. (Photo courtesy of the San Diego Chargers)   See page 47.

As a Chicago Cub, Ken Holtzman achieved his accomplishments the hard way—handing the legendary Sandy Koufax his last regular season defeat before pitching no-hitters at an Atlanta Braves team featuring Hank Aaron and a Cincinnati Reds team featuring Johnny Bench. (Photo courtesy of the Chicago Cubs)

When eleven Israeli athletes were murdered in Munich in 1972, Shep Messing was there as a member of the United States Olympic team. (Photo courtesy of the New York Cosmos, by Alan Tepper) **See page 110.**

HENRY BENJAMIN GREENBERG
DETROIT A.L.1933 TO 1946
PITTSBURGH N.L.1947
ONE OF BASEBALL'S GREATEST RIGHT-HANDED
BATTERS. TIED FOR MOST HOME RUNS BY
RIGHT-HANDED BATTER IN 1938-58. MOST
RUNS-BATTED-IN 1935-37-40-46, AND HOME
RUNS 1938-40-46. WON 1945 PENNANT ON
LAST DAY OF SEASON WITH GRAND SLAM
HOME RUN IN 9TH INNING. PLAYED IN 4
WORLD SERIES, 2 ALL-STAR GAMES. MOST
VALUABLE A.L. PLAYER TWICE-1935-1940.
LIFETIME BATTING AVERAGE .313.

Although he retired in 1947 and a former player becomes eligible for induction into the National Baseball Hall of Fame after only five years out of the game, it was not until 1956 when Hank Greenberg gained the required number of votes to gain entrance. (Photo courtesy of the Detroit Tigers)

DOLPH SCHAYES

"There aren't enough Jews in sports. But, Jewish athletes do perform a valuable public relations service for American Jews.

"Obviously, American Jews take pride in accomplishments of successful Jewish athletes, not only on a national level but down the line in high school.

"Public opinion is influenced by attention getters—whether they be athletes, clergymen or politicians—speaking intelligently on any issue.

"Prejudice, for the most part, has left the American sports scene at all levels. In fact, most teams are on the lookout for Jewish athletes. There is no terrorism threat to a Jewish athlete competing in the United States." (Photo courtesy of the Buffalo Braves)

See page 44.

Roby Young was a former Israeli Olympic Captain, in 1968, and also a member of the Israel National teams from 1962 through 1966 before playing in New York. (Photo courtesy of the New York Cosmos, by Paul Bereswill)

MARILYN RAMENOFSKY (On Right)
(Photo courtesy of the International Swimming Hall of
Fame, by Isadore Wasserman)
See page 81.

SANDY KOUFAX

The greatest pitcher in the history of baseball. See page 36.

STEVE STONE

Steve won the American League Cy Young Award in 1980. See page 87.
(Photo courtesy of the Chicago White Sox)

While the Babe Ruth versus Hank Greenberg question regarding who was the greatest remains unanswered because of Greenberg's five years out of the game in combat during the prime of his career, it would be fair to conclude that Ruth was the greatest left-handed hitter and Greenberg was the greatest right-handed hitter of all time. Here, in 1974, Greenberg is shown with the second greatest right-handed hitter of all time—Joe DiMaggio. (Photo courtesy of Schenley Affiliated Brands Corporation)

Although he slugged 44 home runs in 1946, Hank Greenberg was waived out of the league the following season to the Pittsburgh Pirates where he closed out his career as America's first $100,000 per year athlete. Just as he had said in closing out his nearly successful chase of Babe Ruth's single season home run record in 1938—with what would become a famous concession line, much like Heavyweight Boxing Champion Jack Dempsey's "Honey, I forgot to duck" that President Ronald Reagan recited after being shot—it would have been fitting then for Hank Greenberg to have said for the last time: "That's all right, George, this is as far as I can go too." (Photo courtesy of the Pittsburgh Pirates)

(Photo courtesy of Indianapolis Motor Speedway Corporation)

PETER REVSON

One of the foremost racing car drivers in the world. (See page 102)

GOODY ROSEN

In 1945, Goody Rosen stroked nearly 200 hits for a .325 batting average on his way to a .291 lifetime mark with the Brooklyn Dodgers and New York Giants. But, it was his defensive play as an outfielder that gained him prominence. Although considered small by major league baseball standards, he supplied surprising power on occasion. His career spanned between 1937 and 1945—during which time his successful style of playing shallow and darting back to swoop after fly balls in the outfield became imitated by other major leaguers. In the fifties, Red Sox centerfielder Jimmy Piersall became the ultimate Goody Rosen with that style.

In 1938, *Goody Rosen* was the National League's leading defensive outfielder.

MARTY FLECKMAN

Marty Fleckman earned more recognition as an amateur golfer than as a professional. As an amateur, he captured headlines for stunning upset victories over the biggest name professionals on tour. In Fleckman's first tournament as a professional, he won the 1967 Cajun Classic. But, the rest was downhill; he never regained the classic stroke that had propelled him into prominence from a college campus. For years, Marty was a respected professional, but he never emerged as the super star the press predicted.

Text of Letter from Marty Fleckman To This Author, Dated July 3, 1973

"I am aware of a Jewish following and I enjoy meeting Jewish people all over the world. I really do not feel like Jewish athletes have any special obligation as a spokesman about critical Jewish issues any more than anyone else. It really depends on how strongly they feel about current issues and if they think they can do anything about them.

"I do think the past is past and should be forgotten—if not forgotten, not elaborated on. The Munich tragedy is a definite threat to American Jewish athletes. I would be apprehensive to participate in many countries and I'm sure others will be also. It must be remembered that this did not happen in America.

"I have never encountered prejudice, therefore, it has played no part in my career. I sincerely believe most American Jews cannot complain about prejudice in the USA. Religion really has not played any part in my career as I can see, except for the special following by Jewish fans that cheer me on.

"My goal is to be successful in my chosen profession. Accomplishments come with living and I've had many already. I graduated from college, I'm following my chosen profession and I'm looking forward to my greatest accomplishment."

(Photo courtesy of the Tournament Players Division of the Professional Golfers' Association of America)

AARON KRICKSTEIN

When Aaron Krickstein defeated Henrik Sundstrom to capture the Israel Tennis Center Classic at Tel Aviv in 1983—just two months after his sixteenth birthday—he became the youngest player to win a Grand Prix tournament. The year also saw Krickstein power his way past Vitas Gerulaitis in the Round of 16, U.S. Open, at Flushing Meadow, New York to become the youngest male player to reach the fourth round of the U.S. Open. The following year, he emerged as the youngest player in history to attain a top 10 ranking.

The September 3, 1984 issue of *People* magazine quotes Svengali Nick Bollettieri, Krickstein's coach, as attributing the fact that "Aaron was brought up in a Jewish background and babied for 16 years." In the March 1985 issue of *Monthly Detroit*, writer Terry Kahn succinctly captured Krickstein's tennis game: "He tends to stay back at the baseline, content for the most part to hit looping backhands and flat forehands deep, waiting for an opponent to dish up a weak return. Then Aaron tees off with his tremendous forehand. . ." In the May 27, 1988 *International Tennis Weekly,* managing editor Michael Curet likened Krickstein's career to a roller-coaster ride. According to Curet: "Unexpected injuries appeared and reappeared, jolting the young star, knocking him out of a No. 7. ATP ranking, and making the comeback trail that much more difficult." On September 5, 1988, in the fourth round of the U.S. Open, former Wimbledon champion Stefan Edberg fell in defeat to Krickstein, then ranked number twenty-three and on his way back up.

EADIE WETZEL

In 1968, Eadie Wetzel would surface as swimming's National 200-meter Freestyle Champion and world record holder; she would later be inducted into the International Swimming Hall of Fame.

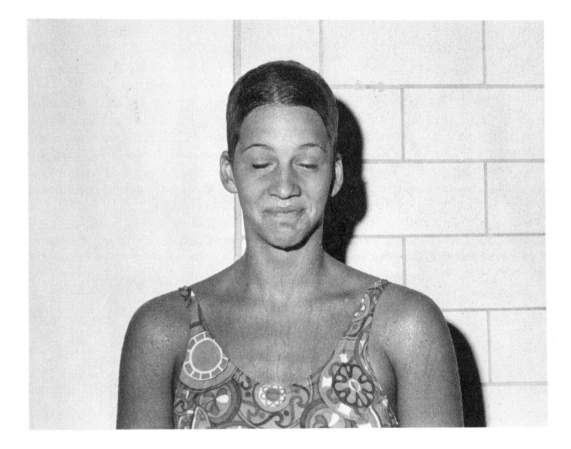

Eadie Wetzel beams after breaking the world record for the 200-meter freestyle. (Photo courtesy of the International Swimming Hall of Fame)

MARTIN JAITE

His membership on the Argentinian Davis Cup team and residence in Barcelona, Spain, has led many to the erroneous conclusion that he was of another religion than Jewish. But a source from his representative ProServ agency double-checked and later confirmed the story related to me by a public relations practitioner of another agency that Martin Jaite is indeed. If this fact had been widely known in 1986, then Jaite's Forest Hill victory over German star Boris Becker that year as a semifinalist might have generated added attention similar to that afforded the victories by Brad Gilbert. Ironically, the September 26, 1986 *International Tennis Weekly* quoted Jaite with reference to his record of playing exceptionally well in Germany, as having said: "I always seem to feel good and do well in Germany." No mention was made of the significance that less than half a century ago, his fate in that country would have been different. As an Argentian Jew, rumors that Nazis such as Martin Gormann might be living in his country with the protection of its government offer Martin Jaite a rare opportunity to emerge as a Jewish hero by exerting his visibility to speak out.

Martin Jaite came away as champion of the Spanish Satellite Circuit in 1983, the Curitiba Challanger at Brazil in 1984, the Grand Prix de Verano at Buenos Aires in 1985, the Bologna Masters in 1986, the Mercedes Cup at Stuttgart in 1986, the Kim Top Line Grand Prix at Palermo in 1987, and the Court of Godo Cup at Barcelona the same year.

STEVE TANNEN

He emerged in the seventies out of the school of Ron Mix—the Intellectual Assassin of the previous decade—but injuries would constrain Steve Tannen from capturing superstardom in the National Football League, despite the fact he played in New York. An All-America defensive cornerback at the University of Florida with a habit of blocking punts and kicks, he would surface as a number-one draft choice of the New York Jets. But the one-time high school track superstar turned poet, played hurt through most of his still brilliant professional career. Steve would eventually find a home with the Jets at free safety, where he led the team in interceptions in 1972—when Jewish athletes died in Munich. His fearless suicide squad play earned Tannen a reputation as one of the most feared tacklers in the game. But, it was the Tannen speed that enabled him to make the big play—which would become his trademark.

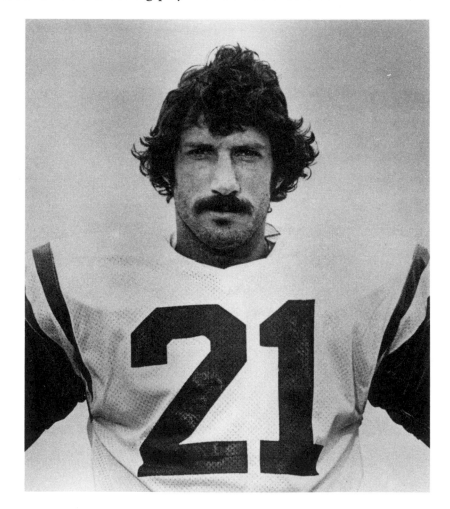

Steve Tannen earned distinction as a fierce tackler and frequent interceptor. (Photos courtesy of the New York Jets)

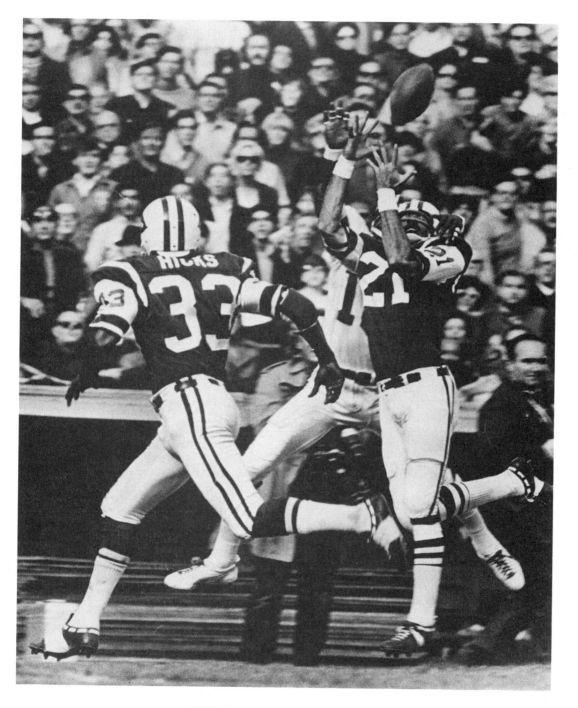

STEVE TANNEN

ELIOT TELTSCHER

In February 1979—not long after his nineteenth birthday—an unheralded Jewish tennis player knocked the number four named player in the world out of the second round of a Palm Springs tournament. That number four ranked player was John McEnroe; and he was on his way to a long reign as number one. The Jewish player was Eiot Teltscher. Four years later, Teltscher would do it again on his own way to becoming a semifinalist of the Volvo Masters in New York. The former UCLA All-America eventually soared to a ranking as high as number 6 in the world in May of 1982. Teltscher was a quarterfinalist at the U.S. Open in 1980, 1981, and 1983—a year in which he was also a semifinalist as the Australian Open and a round of 16 finisher at the French Open. He compiled championships in the Seiko Super Tournament at Hong Kong in 1987 and 1988, the GWS Mazda Classic at Brisbane in 1984, the Altech South African Open at Johannesburg in 1984, the Japan Open at Tokyo in 1983 over Andres Gomez, the TransAmerica Open at San Francisco in 1981, the San Juan Tennis Classic in 1981, the *Atlanta Journal-Constitution* Open in 1979 and 1980, and the Island Holidays Tennis Classic at Maui in 1980.

AMOS MANSDORF

After starring as a member of the Israeli Olympic team in 1984, Amos Mansdorf joined the United States Tennis Association and immediately advanced in the rankings toward the top ten tennis players in the world. Between play on the Israeli Davis Cup team, Mansdorf burst into prominence as champion of the Altech Open, in Johannesburg, South Africa, in 1986; and then as champion of the Riklis Israel Tennis Center Classic, in Tel Aviv, in 1987. He was finalist in the 1987 Vienna Grand Prix, in Austria, after having gained considerable press coverage for his competitive drive.

NORMAN SPER, JR.

Young, gifted and Jewish: Norman Sper, Jr. earned induction into the International Swimming Hall of Fame by winning the National Diving Championship in 1944, 1945 and 1949.

THE JEWISH-AMERICAN ALL-TIME ATHLETIC RANKINGS

The Fifth Jewish Supreme Fourteen

(tie) 57. Morrie Arnovich
(tie) 57. Elise Burgin
58. Mike Epstein
59. Ross Brooks
60. Ron Blomberg
61. Danny Schayes
62. Richie Scheinblum
63. Jay Berger
64. Art Shamsky
65. Ernie Grunfeld
66. Bo Belinsky
67. Donald Cohan
(tie) 68. Joel Kramer
(tie) 68. Shlomo Glickstein
69. Norm Miller
(tie) 70. Janet Haas
(tie) 70. Mike Veisor

MORRIE ARNOVICH

He had batted as high as .324 and had been selected to a National League All-Star team. He had a career batting average close to .300 and was considered one of the most reliable outfielders in baseball. But, after World War II broke out, he was out of baseball in military service for four years—four years of his prime. From a career that began in 1939 and ended with four years of military service at his peak, Arnovich retired in 1946 with a .287 lifetime batting average and unanswered questions regarding how much better he could have been had he not lost those four years.

ELISE BURGIN

One of the great doubles tennis players in history, Elise Burgin has shared championships with Ros Fairbank at the 1987 Virginia Slims of New England in Worcester, the 1986 Eckerd Open in Largo, and the 1986 Egbaston Classic in Birmingham; with Pam Shriver at the 1987 Virginia Slims of Washington in Fairfax; with B. Nagelson at the 1986 European Open in Lugano; with Martina Navratilova at the Virginia Slims of Houston in 1986, where she also scored a finalist finish in singles play with victories over Manuela Maleeva and Zina Garrison; with Kathy Horvath at the Virginia Slims of Indianapolis in 1985; and with Linda Gates at the NCAA Tournament in 1984. In 1986, she won her first professional singles title by capturing the Wild Dunes Invitational in Charleston. As a four-time All-America at Stanford, Burgin shared the Junior Award for Academic Excellence with a male athlete who would also go on to stardom as a professional. His name was John Elway. In the November 23, 1986 *Baltimore Sun,* correspondent Abby Karp filed this report on how Elise Burgin described her own style: "The 5-foot-5 left-hander describes her game as a combination of styles—'serve and volley, serve and stay back; top spin, flat, slice.'"

Elise Burgin

MIKE EPSTEIN

Mike Epstein and Gerry Cooney performed at different times and in different sports. In the late sixties through early seventies, Epstein played first base for five baseball teams. About five years after Epstein retired, Cooney launched a career as a heavyweight boxer that stretched out almost as long a period as Epstein's baseball career. Epstein and Cooney had remarkably similar careers.

Both men were of ethnic groups that were not represented in their sports in proportion to their numbers in society. Very few Jewish men played Major League baseball; and very few white men boxed in the heavyweight division. Both Epstein and Cooney were enormous physical specimens—much larger than most of their competitors. Both Epstein and Cooney began their careers with spectacular success against dubious opposition—Epstein against minor league pitching and Cooney against boxers who were old relative to their sport. Both Epstein and Cooney drew early career comparisons with legendary participants in their sports—Epstein with Hank Greenberg and Cooney with Rocky Marciano, even though Epstein batted from the other side of the plate and Cooney had a completely different style. Both Epstein, who slugged 30 home runs for the 1969 Washington Senators and a team-leading 26 for the 1972 World Champion Oakland A's, and Cooney had respectable careers—but careers that were considered failures because neither achieved greatness.

In 1972, Epstein joined Ken Holtzman and Richie Scheinblum in wearing black armbands to protest the Munich mutilation of that year's Israeli Olympic Team by Arab terrorists.

The six-foot-four-inch and 225-pound Mike Epstein created an awesome sight both at bat and on the field. In his eight-year career, Epstein played for five teams—including the Washington Senators under Ted Williams for whom he slugged 30 home runs in 1969, and for the 1972 World Champion Oakland A's who he led in home runs with 26.

(Photo courtesy of the California Angels)

MIKE EPSTEIN

ROSS BROOKS

Donald Ross Brooks played the toughest position in the National Hockey League—the goal. One of the most brutal, although not the best, hockey players: Brooksie proved himself as capable of making spectacular game-winning saves despite crippling injuries. After ten years of kicking around in senior hockey and minor pro Leagues and even getting his unconditional release at one stage, Ross Brooks made it to the National Hockey league Boston Bruins; for his efforts, he emerged as Rhode Island's Jewish Athlete of the Year. The Rhode Island tough guy never tasted the glory of superstardom; but he had his moments, including a spectacular unbeaten stretch of 13 games.

RON BLOMBERG

He could run; but, he could not judge a fly ball. He could throw; but, the ball tended to get away. And he could hit—and at times really hit; but he never hit consistently for power or even competently against left-handed pitching. Appropriately so, Ron Blomberg became the first designated hitter shortly after the rule was adopted. Ron Blomberg was an enormously successful high average hitter against right-handed pitching in the early seventies whose career ended prematurely because of injury.

Blomberg never was able to take advantage of the short right field fence at Yankee Stadium; and never able to follow the flight of the ball against left-handers without bailing out as he swung. Although he did retire with a nearly .300 batting average, his extraordinary potential went unfulfilled. From the time Mickey Mantle retired until Don Mattingly came along, only Ron Blomberg among the Yankees had the superstar potential to carry the team with consistent high-average power hitting. But, it was unfortunately not to be.

Ron Blomberg's New York Jewish following helped make him one of the most popular Yankees in the post-Mickey Mantle era. (Photos courtesy of the New York Yankees)

RON BLOMBERG
First Base

RON BLOMBERG

This rare shot of two Jewish baseball players in action shows Rom Blomberg darting back to first as Mike Epstein awaits the pickoff attempt. (Photo courtesy of the California Angels, by Sam Spine)

DANNY SCHAYES

The name of his father, Dolph Schayes, can be found in this Jewish Sports Hall of Fame as one of the Jewish Magnificent Seven. But Danny Schayes has made it on his own account. The exact time at which basketball center Danny Schayes emerged from his father's shadow may have come sooner. However, the earliest national documentation is found in the March 24, 1981 *New York Times*. The headline read: "Injured Dan Schayes Is Indispensable Man." Not once in the feature length article did reporter Gerald Eskenazi make reference to his father Dolph. It was the basketball accomplishments of Danny Schayes that had earned him national attention. The nearly seven-foot center played his college career at Syracuse University—in the same city where his father became a legend with the old Syracuse Nationals. In the *Times* article, Danny Schayes described his own playing style: "I'm a role player—get the rebound out for the fast break. Then I come down trailing the play and look for the jump shot if its open." At Syracuse, Schayes was named First-Team All-Big East and an Honorable Mention All-America. He played for the gold medal United States teams in the 1977 and 1981 Maccabiah Games in Israel. He entered the National Basketball Association as a high first-round draft choice of the Utah Jazz, but did not experience success until a trade to the Denver Nuggets placed him on a fast breaking team compatible with his running style for whom he could provide some much needed inside muscle.

DANNY SCHAYES

RICHIE SCHEINBLUM

In 1972, Richie Scheinblum led the American League in hitting for most of the season and earned a berth on the All-Star team. But, it was when eleven Israeli athletes were murdered by Arab terrorists in the Munich Olympics that year—it was then—that Richie Scheinblum made the Jewish Sports Hall of Fame. He risked his life by setting himself up as a potential terrorist target with a black band around his uniform sleeve, much like the one worn by Ken Holtzman and Mike Epstein, and made public statements condemning the murders. Richie Scheinblum had suddenly gained visibility as the leading hitter in the American League; and he used it to call attention to another Jewish tragedy.

Text of Letter from Richie Scheinblum To This Author, Dated June 5, 1973

In a letter to me postmarked June 5, 1973, Richie Scheinblum reflected upon the Munich murders and his reaction to it.

"I feel I have a Jewish following and I feel representative of a lot of people.

"When the 11 athletes were murdered in Munich, I felt it hit home; I wore the emblematic black band, which I felt was very important—not only because they were Jewish athletes, but because they were human beings. I made some of my feelings known in print and did afterwards feel there would be a threatening response. But, nothing was said.

"My goal is to be given a chance to play."

Richie Scheinblum—Anatomy of a Smooth-Swinging, Switch-Hitter. (Photos courtesy of the Kansas City Royals)

RICHIE SCHIENBLUM

JAY BERGER

The former Clemson University All America tennis player came into his own in 1986 as champion of the USTA Satellite, West Palm Beach, and the prestigious Buenos Aires Grand Prix, Argentina. In 1985, Berger had won the National Junior Championship, Kalamazoo; the Florida State Junior Championship; and the National Junior Clay Court Championship, Louisville. In 1987, he went down as a finalist, semifinalist, or quarterfinalist in four tournaments. He gained recognition as one of the top clay court players in tennis.

ART SHAMSKY

Chronic back miseries constrained the awesome power of Art Shamsky. But, Major League Baseball would enter his name into its record books along with a host of superstars when he slugged four home runs in four consecutive trips to the plate; and Art did it the hard way. He hit three of them on August 12, 1966, after entering a 13-inning game as a pinch hitter; two days later, Art hit the fourth—also as a pinch hitter. His bad back, however, would relegate him to part-time duty throughout his career.

(Photo courtesy of the New York Mets)

ERNIE GRUNFELD

As a Scholastic Coach first team All America, Grunfeld became the first high schooler to make the United States basketball team for the Maccabiah Games; he would later emerge as the United States' Most Valuable Player. At the University of Tennessee, the rugged Romanian-Jew drew acclaim as an exceptional shooter and extraordinary offensive rebounder; while he didn't have the grace of a Dolph Schayes, Ernie took the ball to the basket with fierce authority. Unfortunately, he also didn't have the size for that style of play to follow Shayes's footsteps into professional basketball super stardom. However, he closed out his pro career as a valuable role player with the New York Knicks, where he later caught on as a broadcaster.

At Tennessee, Ernie Grunfeld starred on the offensive boards. Grunfeld closed out his professional career with the New York Knicks, with whom he served as a valuable role player. (Photo courtesy of the University of Tennessee)

BO BELINSKY

Son of a Jewish mother and Polish father, Robert "Bo" Belinsky did what came naturally to Jewish left-handed baseball pitchers: he threw a no-hitter. But unlike a Sandy Koufax or a Kenny Holtzman, Bo Belinsky never made it a practice to stay in condition. After his no-hitter, he self-destructed. And unlike a Koufax or a Holtzman, Belinsky pitched only one no-hitter and never drew recognition as a Major Leaguer. Still, Bo Belinsky compiled a record he could brag about; and he did. A book published sometime after his retirement told all the details of his dealings with such Hollywood starlets as Mamie Van Doren, Tina Louise and Ann-Margret and his marriage with once *Playboy* Playmate of the Year, Jo Collins. In the Dial Press' 1973 book—*Bo: Pitching and Wooing* by Maury Allen and Bo Belinsky—Belinsky was quoted as saying: "I don't feel sorry for myself; I've been in the sun."

(Photo courtesy of the California Angels)

Bo Belinsky

DONALD COHAN

Yachting champion Donald Cohan was a member of the 1972 United States Olympic team and a bronze medal winner in Kiel, Germany. Cohan participated in the 1968, 1972, 1976, 1980, and 1984 Olympic Trials; he was participating as a finalist in the 1988 Olympic Trials. He represented the United States in 13 Olympic class World Championships. He has been United States, East Coast, West Coast, Chesapeake Bay Champion in various Olympic classes. Cohan served as a member of the United States Committee for Yachting.

In a letter to me dated May 27, 1987, Donald Cohan expressed definitive opinions regarding his experiences as a Jewish athlete. As a medalist in the tragic 1972 Munich Olympics in which eleven members of the Israeli team were murdered on German soil by Arab terrorists, Cohan—as many Jewish people did—took exception to International Olympic Committee President Avery Brundage's refusal to honor Israel's plea to halt those games after her athletes and coaches were slain.

Text of Letter from Donald Cohan To This Author, Dated May 27, 1988

"As one who has participated in a great many sports at rather high levels, I think that a top Jewish athlete has the additional burden of acting in a manner that brings credit to 'his people.' Most other athletes do not have this additional burden.

"I was the first Jew to make the U.S. Olympic Team in yachting and the first one in the world to win an Olympic medal in yachting. In various Olympic class racing (the toughest of all), I have been Chesapeake Bay Champion, twice Pacific Coast Champion, U.S. Champion, third in the Worlds and have represented the United States in thirteen World Championships. I have raced in Sweden, Germany, France, Italy, Australia, Denmark, England, Canada, Puerto Rico, etc.

"Often the world of yachting is that of socially prominent yacht clubs, although this recently has been changing, and, therefore, you must belong to a yacht club before you can enter a regatta.

"There was a sense of the walls tumbling when I appeared and succeeded and the environment was not historically one in which a Jew associated. As a graduate of Amherst College and Harvard Law School, frankly I felt quite comfortable within myself, although at times I sensed that there were those who wished I would go away.

"At a recent World Championship, I was asked if being Jewish caused me to have a different attitude toward my competitive approach. Frankly, I think it does and although I am quite competitive to start with, there is always that little tug in the back of my mind that drives me to be the last one to throw in the towel. We are all complicated people and I am as 'assimilated' as any athlete there is. At times, I think this puts extra pressure on me, who is so well accepted, knowing that being Jewish requires me to hold to the highest of standards. I don't think this is a burden and I think in the long run has been a very good guide and anchor for me.

"Another factor that pressures me is that I am 57 years old, twice as old as most of my competitors, one of the few amateurs at a world-class level and I have very little time to sail since I have a rather overly full life—yet I won the Atlantic Coast

Championship last year and I leave June 18th to race in Germany in the Soling World Championship.

"Another interesting fact that might intrigue you was that the last official act of that no good son-of-a-witch anti-Semitic Avery Brundage was to hang an Olympic medal around my neck in Germany in 1972—the first time that Germany had the Olympics since Hitler put his show on in 1936."

Photo courtesy of Donald Cohen

JOEL KRAMER

In the Western Conference Finals of the National Basketball Association playoffs in 1979, a six-foot-seven-inch and 218-pound rookie came off the bench to replace the starting center who had been injured. He led his team to three straight wins and the series. Although Joel Kramer scored 19 points for the Phoenix Suns in game six of that series, it was amazing defensive play against a much taller opponent that sealed the victories. Kramer contributed five years as a valuable role player for the Suns.

(Photo courtesy of the Phoenix Suns)

SHLOMO GLICKSTEIN

Shlomo Glickstein crashed the top 30 tennis rankings in 1981, thus becoming the first genuine star from Israel in that sport. From 1976–83, he represented Israel on her Davis Cup team; and in five of those years, he won the Israeli National Championship. Among his victories include a 1980 upset of top 10 player Paul Ramirez at Wimbledon, a 1980 win over Illie Nastase at Tel Aviv, and a 1985 defeat of Balaza Tarcozy in the Davis Cup. He was champion of the Australian Hardcourt Championships in 1980, the Mutual Benefit Life Open in 1981, and the Israel Open in 1983.

NORM MILLER

A good-field-no-hit outfielder, Norm Miller earned his reputation as one of Major League Baseball's most flamboyant individuals by being in the right place at the right time. With the Houston Astros, Norm roomed with Jim Bouton while Bouton was writing his shocking best-seller *Ball Four*. And with the Atlanta Braves, his locker was next to Henry Aaron's the year Aaron chased after and finally caught up with Babe Ruth's homerun record.

In a letter to me postmarked April 29, 1973, Norm Miller reflected upon the implications of the Munich murders.

Letter from Norm Miller To This Author, Dated April 29, 1973

"I think at the time of the tragedy at Munich, my feeling and emotions were concern as a person—rather than a Jew. Don't misunderstand me: it was just that I felt no matter what religious preference or nationality of the people involved, it was a universal disaster—not just a blast on Jews.

"As for it affecting me personally: I feel no threat to myself or future opportunities of Jews in sports."

An acrobatically spectacular defensive outfielder, Norm Miller also posed a dangerous threat as a pinch hitter—batting .323 in that capacity in 1973.

(Photo courtesy of Janet Haas)

JANET HAAS

Her proudest personal accomplishment came when she received a silver medal in the Ninth Maccabiah Games tennis finals; she had been seeded sixth in her first international competition, so her second place finish was considered a surprise. Janet Haas also received a bronze medal in the tennis doubles. Although she didn't play tennis until age 14, Haas emerged from the University of Miami as one of the greats in collegiate women's tennis history. As a professional, she maintained a balanced game—equally comfortable at the baseline or at the net. In a letter to me postmarked December 7, 1973, this is what Janet Haas wrote on the subject of Jews in sports:

Letter from Janet Haas To This Author, Dated December 7, 1973

"During my trip to Israel to participate in the Ninth Maccabiah Games, I learned Jewish athletes perform a valuable public relations service for American Jews. Since in most sports the Jewish athlete is in the minority, he or she has a special drive and desire to be the best. As they are making themselves known, other Jews take pride in reading and hearing about them. When other Jews see what Jewish athletes are accomplishing, it gives them a certain feeling of pride.

"I have noticed when a Jewish athlete accomplishes a great feat, other Jews mention his accomplishment as well as his Jewishness in one sentence. Meaning, they recognize what the athlete has done is tremendous and boast about him because he is a Jew, which fills them with pride.

"Jewish athletes most certainly should use their prominence to exert influence on public opinion about critical Jewish issues. I feel they should know their subject perfectly and discuss it with their Rabbi or other knowledgable Jews before making a public statement. Like many Black athletes: the Jewish athlete can contribute to influencing other Jews to act on matters, such as the Mid-East crisis.

"From my own personal experience, I would say Jewish athletes feel the sting of prejudice more than other Jews. I was brought up in a Jewish community and never knew of such prejudices until I played on a national tennis circuit. Many clubs were anti-Semitic. They did not let Jews join or play at the club. Since I was there as a participant in a tournament, they had no choice. I sometimes had the feeling people were saying: 'The Jewish girl on court five is winning.' Jewish athletes feel prejudice more than other Jews because they are in the public eye.

"Jewish athletes face a threat of terrorism nonexistent to other athletes. Not only from my own experience but from history, I believe there is a threat on Jewish athletes. Before I left for Israel to participate in the Maccabiah Games, the United States team met in New York. Security was unbelievable. Police and undercover agents lined the hotel. They escorted us on buses and on the flight. Obviously, there was a threat because we were Jewish athletes—not just athletes, but athletes that were Jewish. What happened in Moscow during the World Intercollegiate Games was appalling. The Israeli team was booed and stoned. They again were not looked upon as gifted athletes, but as Jews—different from the rest."

MIKE VEISOR

Mike Veisor hoped to become the first Jewish goalie in the National Hockey League; but, Ross Brooks beat him to the punch, with the rival Boston Bruins. The Chicago Black Hawks finally turned to the small, quick, rugged goalie from Canada and the National Hockey League had two Jewish goalies.

(Photo courtesy of the Chicago Black Hawks)

THE JEWISH-AMERICAN ALL-TIME SPORTS EXECUTIVE RANKINGS

1. Barney Dreyfuss
2. Red Auerbach
3. Harry Glickman
4. Edward Rosenblum
5. Max Winter
6. Abe Pollin
7. Art Modell
8. Irv Mondshein
9. Abe J. Greene
10. Carroll Rosenbloom
11. Sid Gillman
12. Al Davis
13. Gabe Paul
14. Al Schacht
15. Red Holzman
16. Allie Sherman
17. Sonny Werblin
18. Red Sarachek
19. Roy Rubin
20. (tie) Arthur Tauber
20. (tie) Norman Bramam

BARNEY DREYFUSS

One of the most successful executives in Major League Baseball history, Barney Dreyfuss also tried his hand at owning a football team—a champion team, no less. But, it was baseball that inscribed Barney's name on a special honor roll for executives in its Hall of Fame. The World Series was Barney Dreyfuss's brainchild; he, alone, conceived it. Until Babe Ruth turned the New York Yankees into the Bronx Bombers, Barney Dreyfuss's Pittsburgh Pirates were considered by many to be baseball's most succesful dynasty. He built the Pirates from scratch; in 31 years, his team won two World Series, six pennants and finished in the first division 25 times.

(Photo courtesy of Barney Dreyfuss)

(Photo courtesy of the Boston Celtics)

RED AUERBACH

In the decade from 1956 to 1966, the Boston Celtics won nine basketball world championships—eight of them in succession and all under the guidance of Arnold "Red" Auerbach. A fierce competitor, whose run-ins with officials became legendary, Red Auerbach was the National Basketball Association's foremost ambassador; his trips on behalf of the United States State Department took him, literally, to every corner of the globe. His greatest accomplishment was the dynasty he left behind of former players coaching in the professional, collegiate, and high school ranks. It was Red Auerbach who broke the color line by installing the first black head coach of a team in any major professional sport. Auerbach received practically every award that can go to a professional coach, including induction into the Basketball Hall of Fame.

In a letter to me postmarked September 27, 1973, Red Auerbach addressed the impact of Jews in sports.

Text of Letter from Red Auerbach To This Author, Dated September 27, 1973

"I think it is self-explanatory that naturally the Jewish athletes perform a great public relations media for American Jews. I feel that most of the American Jews take pride in the Jewish athletes and their accomplishments because I hear these comments wherever I go. As a matter of fact, they always want to know why there aren't more of them; but, that in itself is another problem.

"As far as Jewish athletes using their prominence to exert influence on public opinion, I think that is strictly an individual situation as to how the athlete himself feels relative to Jewish issues.

"I can't believe that the Jewish athlete feels more prejudice than any other Jew. In fact, I would be of the opinion that—on the whole—there is a great deal less prejudice for the athletes than for Jews in other phases of life. I can't suppose what conditions are in certain parts of the world, but, I am sure in this country the Jewish athlete faces no more threat of terrorism than any other athlete."

HARRY GLICKMAN

As executive vice president of professional basketball's Portland Trail Blazers, Harry Glickman had built a potential dynasty under the philosophy of team synergism. In 1977, synergism prevailed over spectacular individual efforts of Julius Erving and company—the awesome Philadelphia 76ers—when the Trail Blazers romped to an easy title despite the showtime of Dr. J., as Erving was called. Glickman had scientifically built a role playing unselfish supporting cast behind Bill Walton—demonstrably the greatest center ever to play the game—that maximized the impact of Walton's style. Because Walton played a purely unselfish game—relying on defense, outlet passes, and rebounds—the play of each supporting team member was also maximized to the extent that the collective performance of the team exceeded the maximum conceivable cumulative levels of each player individually. Suddenly, Bill Walton suffered career-wrecking stress fractures and the anticipated dynasty crumbled with the bones in his feet.

But, Harry Glickman was used to adversity. Many of his relatives died a torturous death at Treblinka. The May 6, 1985 *New York Times* shows that Glickman used his prominence as a sports celebrity to speak out in support of Jewish interests. As Ronald Reagan insulted world Jewry by placing a wreath in memoriam for the 49 Waffen SS soldiers (and the regular German army soldiers) buried at the Bitburg military cemetery in West Germany, Harry Glickman spoke out. The *Times* noted that Reagan's visit to Bitburg caused the memory of Treblinka to intrude on the Blazers' upset victory in a game over the Los Angeles Lakers that day.

Text of Letter From Edward Rosenblum To This Author, Dated August 21, 1974

"The Jewish-American athlete in association and competition with his non-Jewish athlete was the formation and monumental beginning to better understanding and a more harmonious relationship between the two groups. It was through this association and competition that brought the world's ethnic groups together, proving that race, creed or color is no barrier to meeting as brothers and sisters in sports. The greatest media for human relations and understanding is through competitive sports.

"Through my six decades of affiliation with amateur sports, I have never incurred any animosity because of my being Jewish. And I have officially attended six Olympic Games, two Pan-American Games and countless other games of various sports throughout the world. There is a special mystique about taking part in the Olympic Games that no other competition can approach.

"The Olympics I will remember most were the XXth Olympiad, held in Munich during August and September 1972. A Jewish-American athlete was heralded as the greatest athlete in Munich for his performance as a swimmer; the seven gold medals Mark Spitz won were more than any athlete had ever captured. We all felt these Games would be the best ever held.

"Suddenly—without warning one morning around 5:00—a group of Arab terrorists scaled the Olympic Village fence, near the Israeli cottage. You know the rest of the story. I was called early that morning by a member of the Israeli Olympic Committee and informed of the tragedy. Great pressure from around the world was being used to have the balance of those Olympic Games cancelled; telegrams by the thousands were received by the Olympic Committee. Following burial of the heroic Israeli athletes, Israeli Prime Minister Golda Meir telephoned Olympic officials and requested that the Games continue. Because thousands of young men and women had trained four years to compete, the former prime minister felt the Games must go on. The Games resumed, but without much enthusiasm.

"One of my proudest accomplishments was the part I played with the late Colonel Harry Henshel and Charles Ornstein as members of the Executive and Foreign Relations Committee of the Amateur Athletic Union of the United States and the United States Olympic Committee; we paved the way for presentation of the membership application of the newly-formed Israel Olympic Committee to the International Olympic Committee. Avery Brundage, then President of the International Olympic Committee, interceded on behalf of Israel's request for admission and used his influence with his colleagues to vote their admission. After a battle royal with the Arab and African national representatives, Israel was admitted in 1954. I might add—with considerable pride—that I have witnessed the performance of the Israel Olympic teams in competition since their admission to the Games; they have progressed immensely.

"During the past sixty years, I have served with a great deal of pleasure in many Jewish activities as well as amateur sports. I hope to continue with these same interests as long as I live. Amateur sports is far more than just an entertainment show; and Jewish boys and girls have made a splendid contribution."

(Photos courtesy of Edward Rosenblum)

EDWARD ROSENBLUM

A pioneer member of the Amateur Athletic Association and founder of the Jewish Community Center of Washington, D.C., Edward Rosenblum's most memorable accomplishment was organizing the first visit ever by a United States track and field team to Russia in 1958. He was on the United States Olympic Committee at the Tokyo and Mexico City olympiads; then, Edward Rosenblum saw bitter memories of the Holocaust revived. Edward Rosenblum had traveled to Germany with the United States Olympic Committee in 1972, only to be at the scene of another atrocity. Still a swimmer and handball player in his eighties, he would pause only long enough to receive awards—awards that date back to 1923 for relief efforts as a representative of the American Jewish Joint Distribution Committee in White Russia. The semi-retired attorney devoted 90 percent of his time to the United Jewish Appeal, the Hebrew Home for the Aged, the Jewish Community Center of Greater Washington, the Jewish Home for the Retarded and his synagogue—Washington's Adas Israel Congregation. In a letter to me postmarked August 21, 1974, Edward Rosenblum gave an eyewitness account of the Munich murders.

The American flag arrives in The Soviet Union on a peaceful mission. This same flag announced the U.S.A. team as it entered The Moscow Stadium , July, 1958, applauded by 80,000 Russian spectators.
(Photo courtesy of Edward Rosenblum)

MAX WINTER

Co-owner and general manager of championship teams in professional basketball and football, Max Winter dealt in innovations. His National Basketball Association Minneapolis Lakers won five divisional and two World Championships over a five-year span; his National Football League Minnesota Vikings made return trips to the Super Bowl. Max Winter's champions were giants on and off the field, because Max concentrated on the little things that make athletes feel big. As a young man, Max had been an athlete himself; he was a noted gymnast and ice skater in Austria, before his family sailed for America and a better life. In a letter to me postmarked September 27, 1974, Max Winter conveyed some unusually frank assessments of selected Jewish athletes.

Text of Letter From Max Winter To This Author, Dated September 27, 1974

"As for Jewish athletes using their recognition to benefit their fellow Jews, I do believe that Mr. Spitz had a great opportunity to assert himself on many issues that would have been published around the world.

"As for a comparison of Sid Luckman, Benny Friedman and Harry Newman: it is unfair for me to rank them even though it was fortunate to see them all on several occasions. All three of them were very great quarterbacks and, unless given the same chance on the same teams, I doubt that there could be a great comparison."

(Photo courtesy of the Minnesota Vikings)

ABE POLLIN

Jewish philanthropist Abe Pollin never forgot where he came from, even after his success as a professional basketball team owner earned him selection as chairman of the National Basketball Association's board of governors. The Capital Centre he built in metropolitan Washington, D.C., to house his basketball and hockey teams, was acclaimed as one of the most beautiful facilities in the world. Always a leader in Jewish benefits, he launched a drive to build a memorial at Tel Aviv University for the Israeli athletes slain at the Munich Olympics in 1972. During my interview of him at his office in June of 1973, Abe Pollin talked about the special role of Jewish athletes.

Transcript of Interview of Abe Pollin, in June 1973

"Every Jew has a responsibility to his fellow Jews throughout the world and to Israel because Jews are few in number. When the Israeli athletes were murdered in Munich, I was determined I would do something so the 11 martyrs would never be forgotten. I raised funds to create a memorial for the slain with a sports facility at Tel Aviv University. As an American, a Jew, a person involved with sports and most of all as a human being, I felt the memorial was the most effective thing I could do. This was my way of protest. I think—in his own way—every true Jew did something to show their outrage. The money raised is not just a Jewish effort, but an American effort to show the outrage of every citizen.

"I think it is incumbent on every Jew to recognize when an injustice against humanity has taken place and to enlighten others about that injustice. When that injustice affects only Jews, the burden of informing the rest of the world rests upon the Jewish voice.

"If there ever was a stereotype of a weakling Jew, Israel has certainly demolished that. And Jewish athletes reinforce the message.

"On the basketball court—or on any field of sport—religion plays no role. But, I am not that naive to think what happened in Munich in 1972 couldn't happen again. That's why the memorial at Tel Aviv University means so much to me; now, no one will ever forget."

(Photo courtesy of Abe Pollin)

ART MODELL

President of the National Football League in the late sixties—during the time the sport passed baseball as the country's most popular spectator team sport—and long-time owner and president of the Cleveland Browns, Arthur B. Modell had a heart as big as his reputation. The year was 1962; Modell's Browns were set to unveil that player who comes along once in a lifetime. That player's name was Ernie Davis; he was young, gifted, black and dying. Ernie had acute monocytic leukemia and he didn't know it. *Cleveland Plain Dealer* columnist Chuck Heaton covered the Ernie Davis affair and reflected upon it in a letter to me dated March 1, 1972 as background for research on news suppression I was conducting at the time, comparing the media's treatment of Davis and Vince Lombardi eight years later during the times when both public figures were allowed to die in private.

The big news was that Ernie Davis couldn't crack the All-Star's starting lineup. Was this the same superstar who broke all of the legendary Jimmy Brown's college records, or was this just another overrated Heisman Trophy winner?

Unfortunately, it wasn't as simple as that. A few days before the All-Star game, Ernie was hospitalized with what was reported as a "mysterious blood ailment." That was all we were told.

Ernie Davis would quickly slip out of the spotlight and not be mentioned in the papers again for several months. Something was wrong. Something was terribly wrong.

Chuck Heaton, then a staff correspondent and now a sports columnist of the *Plain Dealer,* covered the Ernie Davis affair from its mysterious start to its tragic finish. Here is the affair as Heaton recollected it in a letter to me dated March 1, 1972:

"We learned in a wire service story about a week before the College All-Star game that Ernie hadn't been feeling well and had been put in the hospital.

"I went up to Chicago the Wednesday before the game and met Art Modell at the airport. If my recollection is correct, it was at that time that he told me that Davis had leukemia. I went to the hospital with him but didn't see Ernie.

"Modell later called the late Frank Gibbons, who was covering the All-Star game for the Press, and me, and asked us to come to his suite. He then asked us not to publicize the nature of the illness because Davis had not been informed.

"We agreed to go along if it was all right with our editors. Gordon Cobbledick was sports editor at the time and I reached him at an Indians' baseball game. He felt that this was the right thing to do.

"The Browns finally announced that he had leukemia some months later, after there was a remission and Ernie was feeling better. In fact, he wanted to play football and this was a matter of contention between Paul Brown and Modell. Brown felt that Davis shouldn't play and Modell was inclined to use him as long as Ernie wanted it that way.

"Before the announcement of the nature of the disease, Davis had been informed. I believe he felt so well at the time that he believed he might lick it.

"It was the following spring—something less than a year after he was hit by the disease—that Ernie became ill again. He entered the hospital and was dead less than a week later.

(Photo courtesy of the Cleveland Browns)

"Modell chartered an airplane and flew a party of players, brass, and newsmen to the funeral in Elmira, New York.

"This was an unusual situation, but I believe the Cleveland newspapers handled it in the only way possible."

In a letter to me postmarked June 7, 1973, Art Modell expressed his thoughts about the relative lack of Jews in sports.

Text of Letter from Art Modell To This Author, Dated June 7, 1973

"I think you can understand that all of us associated with the Browns were shocked at the Munich tragedy, but I don't believe that the professional athlete does feel the sting of prejudice more than anyone else.

"As a matter of fact, I sincerely believe there is a lot more democracy in sports than in other areas of our society. Black athletes and Jewish athletes did very well in professional sports many, many years ago—long before the civil rights movement. I guess that the reason there are not so many professional Jewish athletes stems from the fact that our parents from the time were were very young tried to direct us in the careers of law, medicine and other similar professions. Seriously, you must remember that the Jewish population constitutes a very small part of this country."

IRV MONDSCHEIN

An outstanding trackman at New York University and member of the 1948 United States Olympic team, Irving Mondschein was National Collegiate Athletic Association high jump champion in 1947 and 1948 and held both the indoor and outdoor Intercollegiate Athletic Association records. He was Amateur Athletic Union national champion in the decathlon in 1944, 1946 and 1947 and runner-up in 1948 and 1949. Mondchein also played football at New York. He would spend his later years coaching at the high school and college level.

As track coach at the University of Pennsylvania, Irv Mondshein coached many Jewish athletes to further heights. One such Jewish athlete, both literally and figuratively, was Jeff Fried—who would go on to win a gold medal in Israel at the 1973 Maccabiah Games in the high jump event. Fried credited the influence of Irv Mondshein as inspiring him to keep jumping. When I talked with Jeff Fried on August 3, 1974, he was a medical doctor and wanted to be the first of his profession to jump seven feet. This is what Jeff Fried said:

Remarks by Dr. Jeff Fried—An Irv Mondschein Protégé—On August 3, 1974

"I felt I had a Jewish following in my home town; this was evident by informal feedback I would receive from Jewish people in the area.

"Jewish athletes knock down the stereotype of Jewish people as intellectual and helpless—unable to defend themselves. But, after the Six-Day War, much of the stereotype was broken down anyway.

"If my high jumping had propelled me to national fame, I would have used that fame to speak out on Jewish issues if the issues were relevant to sports. For example: if I had been at the 1973 Student World Games in Russia—in which Jewish athletes were harassed—I definitely would have spoken out. However, I don't think it is appropriate for Jewish athletes to use that prominence earned from sports on social issues not involving sports.

"When I was selected to participate in the Ninth Maccabiah Games in Israel in 1973, the risk of terrorism did not keep me home. I felt I was accomplishing more for world peace by going. I know I risked my life, but I had to go. I just accepted the fact there would be danger.

"The priority of those Maccabiah games was security. Even press coverage before the games was toned down in the name of security. The impact of Munich had left its mark. The games were dedicated to the 11 athletes. There was a wonderful torch lighting memorial at the opening ceremonies. As I entered the Hotel Ramat Aviv, the first thing I saw was an Israeli soldier on the roof with a machine gun. Entry from the outside into the hotel required special passes. Before a bus could leave the hotel, it was inspected for bombs. All bags were checked.

"There aren't many Jewish athletes; so as a Jewish athlete, I've always felt I was representative of a large number of Jews and not just myself."

(Photo courtesy of the University of Pennsylvania)

ABE J. GREENE

The New Jersey State Boxing Commissioner was elected president of the National Boxing Association at the height of the holocaust and served an unprecedented seven years. When Abe J. Greene declined reelection as president, he emerged as the National Boxing Association's national commissioner by acclamation. When the National Boxing Association became the World Boxing Association, history repeated itself. Abe was elected president and then moved on to world commissioner, when the post was created. In 1972, the World Boxing Association would elect Abe J. Greene commissioner for lifetime, again by acclamation. Abe J. Greene gave boxing a face lift; his innovations elevated boxing and restored it as a major sport.

In a letter to me postmarked September 9, 1974, Abe J. Greene conveyed profound recollections about the impact of his Jewish heritage on his career as a boxing commissioner.

Text of Letter From Abe J. Greene To This Author, Dated September 9, 1974

"When the late Abe Simon—mastodonic heavyweight—was preparing to appear in a New Jersey ring, he wore a Jewish star on his ring shorts. I took him aside and directed him to get other shorts or turn his own inside out. Simon demurred, insisting he was proud of his race. I told him he was not boxing as a Jew, that there was no reason he should be cheered or jeered as a Jew and that this went for all credoes. Simon insisted on his right to wear the symbol, whereupon I opened my shirt and pointed to my own prayer shawl. I told Simon I had worn the prayer shawl constantly since boyhood, but not on display. Simon got the point and never again wore the Mogen David. All other religious credal symbols were similarly barred and the ban became universal.

"When Joe Louis was preparing to retire, he called on me to announce his abdication of the title and I—as commissioner—helped him to find a lucrative retirement post by setting up a tournament of leading contenders to determine a new champion.

"Rocky Graziano—now a renowned television thespian—was suspended for life by the New York State commission for a mythical offense. As president of the National Boxing Association, I dissented from the severe penalty—insisting the lifetime ban was a kangaroo verdict. Graziano—as a deadend kid—was being consigned to evil days, so I declined to follow New York's example. I rescued Graziano from several other near-fatal involvements and helped the future middleweight launch the career that carried him to the top.

"I took over as New Jersey State Boxing Commissioner when boxing was being investigated for opprobrious practices. I attempted to restore the sport in the state to a high plane of respectability. In one five-year term, I quietly shelved more than 200 boxers—new and old—but quietly counselling them that they were either over the hill or showed palpable lack of prospects for the future. By speaking with the boxers, I avoided announcement of any suspension to avoid stigmatizing them to their friends as punch-drunk."

(Photo courtesy of *The News*, Paterson, New Jersey)

CARROLL ROSENBLOOM

One of the most dramatic football executives, he built dynasties on the east and west coasts. His Baltimore Colts recorded the best record in the National Football League from 1958 through 1972—the year Carroll sold them for the Rams of Los Angeles, which followed in the Colts' footsteps. Former football great Johnny Unitas said of Carroll Rosenbloom: "He has an insatiable desire and drive to be the best at every undertaking." He played halfback on the University of Pennsylvania's football team and pitched for Penn's baseball team.

In a letter to me postmarked November 9, 1973, Carroll Rosenbloom conveyed recognition of the public relations contribution of famous Jewish athletes.

Text of Letter From Carroll Rosenbloom To This Author, Dated November 9, 1973

"Most Jewish athletes perform a valuable public relations service for American Jews. Certainly, Sandy Koufax did because of his great talent, intelligence, modesty, courage and exemplary behavior.

"While the Jewish athlete faced terrorism in the 1972 Olympics, in professional sports in the United States he obviously does not. Jewish athletes should obey dictates of his own heart as to whether he should or should not use his prominence to exert influence on public opinion on such questions as United States' aid to Israel.

"I have never considered athletes as Jewish, Black, Indian or anything other than persons with varying portions of talent, courage and tenacity."

(Photo courtesy of the Los Angeles Rams)

SID GILLMAN

As a Ohio State University freshman, Sid Gillman played baseball and basketball in addition to football. But after skipping football practice in favor of baseball, he was forced to concentrate on only football thereafter. As an end, Sid was selected to the All-Big Ten Team and made All–America Honorable Mention three years in a row. After a brief fling at professional football, Sidney Gillman emerged as one of pro football's most exciting coaches and prominent executives.

(Photo courtesy of the San Diego Chargers)

AL DAVIS

When professional football's American and National Leagues put an end to their Six-Year War, Al Davis drew acclaim as the driving force who brought the leagues to the conference table; with the merger completed, Davis resigned his American Football post of commissioner. His Raiders, for which he eventually directed as managing partner, produced the best record in professional football over a span of more than a decade. Al—the protégé of Sid Gillman—held the dual positions of head coach and general manager at age thirty-three.

(Photo courtesy of The Los Angeles Raiders)

GABE PAUL

One of the shrewdest traders in major league baseball history: Gabe Paul climbed up executive posts with several teams to chief owner of the Cleveland Indians and finally chief owner of the New York Yankees. He—as most Jews eligible during the Holocaust era—served in the military service during World War II. Before coming into baseball, Gabe worked as a writer and later in public relations. That experience would help him in later years to become one of the most highly respected executives in professional sports.

In a letter to me dated May 29, 1973, Gabe Paul expressed his opinion that athletes face less prejudice than people in other walks of life.

Text of Letter From Gabe Paul To This Author, Dated May 29, 1973

"I don't feel that an athlete feels prejudice as much as any normal person, because in athletics: it is the ability that counts. While there may be some barbs thrown, generally talent determines.

"My reaction to the Munich tragedy was horror. I just could not believe it. We have no fears here for the safety of any of the Jewish players. There is always a risk being in front of the public and all players share that risk.

"I think if you will check statistics, you will find that the number of Jewish athletes on professional teams is very close to their overall percentage of the population of this country."

(Photo courtesy of the New York Yankees)

AL SCHACHT

They called him The Clown Prince of Baseball. For years, he remained in the minor leagues; his pitching record in the minors was spectacular. Not until he had worn his arm out did he get the chance to pitch in the major leagues. While Al enjoyed but moderate success on the mound, he would soon emerge as a comedian with an act that would introduce 25 World Series over a span of more than fifty years in baseball. He was affiliated with numerous Jewish activities, including the Sports Lodge of B'nai B'rith. In a letter to me postmarked August 29, 1974, Al Schacht reflected upon his life.

Text of Letter From Al Schacht To This Author, Dated August 29, 1974

"After several years pitching in the minor leagues, I was sold from the Jersey City club to the Washington club back in 1919. After injuring my arm in 1920, I was sent

(Photo courtesy of Al Schacht)

back to the minors in 1922. I was brought back to the Washington club in 1924 as their third base coach the year we won the World Championship.

"My first engagement as an entertainer in baseball came in 1921, in the World Series between the Yankees and Giants at the Polo Grounds. The show consisted of about 20 minutes of pantomime, only before the game started. In all: I entertained in 25 different World Series and 15 All-Star games.

"During the second world war, I entertained the troops in North Africa, Sicily, the Pacific and other islands. Right after the war, I was in the Philippines and Japan for the occupation troops. In 1952 and 1955, I visited the troops in Korea and Japan. In 1947, I had entertained in Europe. I was never paid for any of my visits to our troops.

"Back in 1937 after stepping out of the American League as coach of the Red Sox, I booked myself as an entertainer in minor and big league clubs throughout the country. I appeared in 150 towns a year until the start of the war in 1941.

"During the war, I went into the restaurant business and was in that business for 25 years. While in the restaurant business, I still made appearances in ball parks and entertained troops.

"I had headlined in vaudeville, back in 1927, 28 and 30. Today: I am semi-retired, having sold my property in New York City where my restaurant was located."

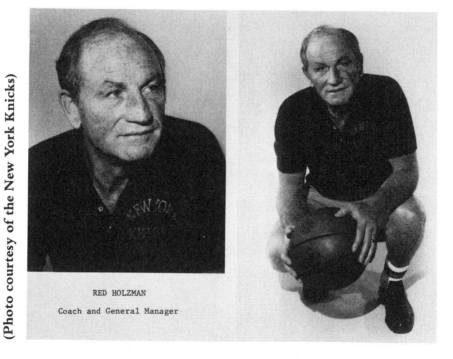

(Photo courtesy of the New York Knicks)

RED HOLZMAN
Coach and General Manager

RED HOLZMAN

Until William Holzman surfaced as a coach of the New York Knickerbockers, the basketball team had been marked with failure; after Red had guided the Knicks to a pair of World Championships—including their first ever—he was elevated to the dual post of general manager-coach. As a player, Red enjoyed moderate success in a bench role.

ALLIE SHERMAN

During the sixties, Allie Sherman went from rags to riches and back to rags again as coach of the New York football Giants; he won the eastern division title from 1961 through 1963 and was named Coach of the Year in both 1961 and 1962. But, by 1968 the Giants were over the hill and Allie was out of work. During the Holocaust and war years, he played quarterback for Brooklyn College and had an undistinguished five-year career as a professional for the Philadelphia Eagles.

(Photo courtesy of the New York Giants, by Bill Mark)

ALLIE SHERMAN
(Photo courtesy of Bill Mark)

SONNY WERBLIN

David A. "Sonny" Werblin—heading a five-man syndicate—purchased a then bankrupt New York American Football League franchise and outbid the established National Football League for the top collegiate talent to force a premature merger between the two leagues. His New York Jets would win the third Super Bowl, between champions of each league. During more than thirty years in show business: Werblin represented such stars as Ed Sullivan, Jackie Gleason, Jack Benny and Andy Williams in their negotiations with television networks and sponsors.

In a letter to me postmarked July 10, 1973, Sonny Werblin expressed a preference for me not to single out Jewish athletes for any special recognition.

Text of Letter From Sonny Werblin To This Author, Dated July 10, 1973

"I have no comment for your book, since as an American, I think there is too much polarization in this country as it is."

(Photo courtesy of the New York Jets)

RED SARACHEK

In 1969—after 26 years as coach of the Yeshiva University basketball team—Bernard "Red" Sarachek stepped aside as coach and devoted himself entirely to the position of athletic director. Red began his long association with basketball in 1926, as a high school player in New York. He would win high school letters in basketball, baseball and football; at New York University, he starred in basketball for three years. After several years of coaching, news of the Holocaust broke out along with World War II. From 1943–45, Red was an American Red Cross field director in the overseas division. Then it was back to basketball coaching. Red's knowledge of the game led to his being named a scout for the New York Nets of the American Basketball Association in 1969, a post he held in addition to his services at Yeshiva.

(Photo courtesy of Yeshiva University)

ROY RUBIN

From athletic director at Long Island University to head coach of the Philadelphia 76ers basketball team in the pros, Roy Rubin was a member of the B'nai B'rith Sports Lodge. Roy's Long Island basketball teams twice won the eastern regionals in the National Collegiate Athletic Association tournament to earn berths in the national finals; in 1968, his Long Island Blackbirds went to the quarterfinals of the National Invitational Tournament. He led a 1971 United States team to third place in the ninth annual Hapoel games in Israel after leading them to the championship in the 1966 Pan American Maccabiah games in Brazil. Roy served as advisor to the 1969 United States team that won the eighth World Maccabiah games in Israel. In high school, Roy Rubin made an All-City team in a city that included Jewish greats Dolph Schayes and Max Zaslofsky and gentile stars Dick McGuire and Bob Cousy. Roy played guard in the National Collegiate Athletic Association tournament in his senior year of college. In a letter to me postmarked September 3, 1974, Roy Rubin commented on the small number of Jews in professional sports:

Text of Letter from Roy Rubin To This Author, Dated September 3, 1974

"There are so few Jews participating in professional sports that a Jewish player or coach provides incentives for those of his race who are so inspired."

(Photo courtesy of Roy Rubin)

NORMAN BRAMAM

Norman Bramam entered sports ownership in the mid-eighties by purchasing the Philadelphia Eagles. It is his recorded willingness to have assumed risks in support of Jewish interests which came before he entered the sports world that—coupled with his position as a sports executive—puts him into the Jewish Sports Hall of Fame. According to the March 8, 1985 *USA Today,* Bramam once "joined picketers protesting a Soviet cellist's concert at the University of Miami." He also paid legal fees for a Jewish activist who released mice to disrupt a Soviet singer's concert. With Norman Bramam in the spotlight by virtue of his position in sports, American Jewry has a receptive channel through which she may convey her collective concerns. Bramam's practice of putting himself on the line for Judaism has earned him distinction.

ARTHUR TAUBER

Arthur D. Tauber completed his college fencing career undefeated. In 1940 and 1941, he was intercollegiate epée champion. Epée is the heaviest weapon, with touches being scored by point only. Tauber was intercollegiate foil champion in 1942. The foil scores by thrusting the point on a limited target. He had coached at Salle Santelli and Sarah Lawrence College, the 1960 United States Olympic fencing team, the 1959 victorious United States Pan American squad, and other institutions before settling in as coach of the fencing team at Yeshiva University.

(Photo courtesy of Yeshiva University)

ABOUT THE AUTHOR

On April 27, 1968—less than two weeks after turning 19—"Buddy" Robert Silverman won a gold medal in weight lifting from the District of Columbia Association of the Amateur Athletic Union of the United States in the 148-pound division. As an animal rights advocate, he emerged as the subject of numerous television and newspaper interviews for his efforts.

As an official in the executive branch of the federal government, he received a rare commendation from the Comptroller General of the United States in 1978, after developing "a model system for oversight of department programs"; and the Secretary of the Treasury Honor Award in 1979, "by identifying and correcting improper and inefficient resource management practices." He was subject of a 1980 *Government Executive* feature article that proclaimed: "What Dr. Silverman has done is to create a survey technique that can isolate the perceived impact of new programs, yet does not fall into a trap of generating the decisions before the fact." In 1981, he received an award from the United States Office of Personnel Management after "developing the innovative concepts for Developmental Pay," which he had introduced in the American Management Associations' *Compensation Review.* Later that year, in the *Journal of Systems Management,* he adapted his pay system to Major League Baseball. Among his other models introduced in professional literature, Dr. Silverman's Optimum Legibility Formula helps to achieve precise writing when it is needed. He appears frequently as a guest speaker.

Silverman received his Doctor of Philosophy degree from the American University after a Master of Arts degree in journalism from Kent State University, where he edited the administration's weekly newspaper in the aftermath of the shooting tragedy there. He published his master's thesis in *College & University Journal* and his doctoral dissertation in *Public Relations Review.* He received his Bachelor of Arts degree from the University of West Florida.

In 1982, he assumed his position as Director of the Naval Facilities Engineering Command Documentation Division in Alexandria, Virginia. He also serves as a primary instructor for the National College of Education out of McLean, Virginia; and as an adjunct professor for the Central Michigan University Institute for Personal and Career Development out of Fairfax, Virginia.

BUDDY ROBERT S. SILVERMAN